The Miracles Of Jesus And Their Flip Side

Cycles A, B, and C

*Miracle narratives
from the Revised Common Lectionary
with a fresh look at the other side of the story*

Jerry L. Schmalenberger

CSS Publishing Company, Inc., Lima, Ohio

THE MIRACLES OF JESUS AND THEIR FLIP SIDE

Library of Congress Cataloging-in-Publication Data

Schmalenberger, Jerry L.
    The miracles of Jesus and their flip side : cycles A, B, and C : miracle narratives from the Revised common lectionary ... / Jerry L. Schmalenberger.
        p. cm.
    ISBN 0-7880-1710-1
    1. Jesus Christ—Miracles—Sermons. 2. Sermons, American. I. Title.
BT366 .S34 2000
252'.041—dc20
                                                                    00-35792
                                                                         CIP

This book is available in the following formats, listed by ISBN:
    0-7880-1710-1   Book
    0-7880-1711-X   Disk
    0-7880-1712-8   Sermon Prep

For more information about CSS Publishing Company resources, visit our website at www.csspub.com.

PRINTED IN U.S.A.

*This book of sermons is dedicated to
the sweet memory of a best friend, classmate, and
brother in Christ, David E. Ullery,
for whom I prayed fervently
a miracle of healing which was not granted.*

Table Of Contents

Foreword

When Dr. Schmalenberger started his semester as a visiting professor at the Augustana Hochschule in Neuendettelsau early this year he told me about his plans to write this book. My first reaction was: it is already such a challenge to preach about only one of the miracle stories, and he is going to write sermons about so many of them.

And now reading the outcome of his endeavor it seems so easy to me to preach about miracles. I learned: you must tell the historical content of a miracle story by translating it into a present-day story. So what's the problem? And even more, the author reveals his recipe, his "simple formula for presenting the miracles in narrative form."

But you may rest assured: the cooking is the problem. As we all know it is a long way from a formula to a sermon, especially to sermons as inspiring as those we read in this book. I presume the *genius loci* of Neuendettelsau had a finger in the pie. By that *genius loci* I mean Wilhelm Loehe who was — besides other talents — a gifted preacher in my little town Neuendettelsau about a century ago.

I can't end this short introduction without a word about the "flip side." In my opinion it's a brilliant idea to look for a fresh approach, a fresh flip side focus in every one of the miracle stories. They tell a lot about the power of the Lord Jesus Christ and therefore the Bible calls them *dynameis*, powerful acts. And as we know from the Bible, Jesus shared this power with his disciples. Should we say that the miracle stories also tell us a lot about those things we are supposed to do as disciples of Jesus? It's you and me who are Side B of the miracles stories, having the chance to be a hit in the charts some time.

Professor Dr. Wolfgang Stegemann
Neuendettelsau, Bavaria
Rektor, Augustana Hochschule

Preface

This little volume of sermons on the miracles of Jesus has been composed at the Franconian village of Neuendettelsau, Germany. Here at the Augustana Hochschule with the luxury of good Bavarian food and rich friendships with faculty colleagues and students, I have wrestled with the Gospel writers' stories of Jesus' astonishing acts of compassion for others.

All the sermons deal with miracles of Jesus now included in the Revised Common Lectionary. There are a few I omitted because of my suspicion they might be the same event told in a little different way. One "raising from the dead" or "driving out demons" miracle seemed sufficient.

This is not an attempt to do an academic examination of these events, but for instruction, inspiration, and preaching. To that end I have tried always to find, in addition to the traditional teaching, a flip side: i.e., an unusual approach to the same story.

This is a companion book to *The Parables of Jesus and Their Flip Side* which is an attempt to do the same treatment of the parables used in the Revised Common Lectionary. It is my hope this fresh approach will also, with the Holy Spirit's help, inspire us as we hear it proclaimed.

In preparing to write these homilies, I have consulted mainly the following authorities:

William Barclay, *The Daily Study Bible* (Philadelphia: Westminster Press, 1956) and *And He Had Compassion* (Edinburgh: St. Andrew Press, 1975).

The Interpreter's One-Volume Commentary (Nashville: Abingdon Press, 1971).

René Latourelle, *The Miracles of Jesus and the Theology of Miracles* (New York: Paulist Press, 1988).

Ronald S. Wallace, *The Gospel Miracles* (Grand Rapids: Wm. B. Eerdmans Publishing Company, 1960).

I'm told that our English word "miracle" comes from the Latin verb *mirari* — to wonder, it moves us to marvel at it. My prayer here in this Bavarian Seminary is that the marvels I found in these graphic stories might move you also to wonder.

Each of the verses of the following poem describes my wonderment and amazement of one of the miracle stories included. The fourth line of each verse reflects the miracle's flip side. The verses appear in the same order as the sermons.

Miracle was a source of power and joy for the first Christians. I hope that will be said of us also.

Life Transformed to Miraculous Grace

Death flutes wailed a morbid tune for Jairus' daughter;
at life's end our graceful God provides for us and loved ones.
By touch old woman's hemorrhage dried up from compassion.
Even when ridiculed, health and wellness is our ministry.

Don't be afraid, the first thought apparition spoke,
across the turbulent waves and strong Galilee wind;
for in the ship of church we are secure with Savior.
And like Peter, we must willingly jump in to assist.

The fulfilled life of discipleship is constant gratitude,
knowing the marvelous grace-gift God has tendered,
to heal us of our maladies and natural sinfulness.
We are to care for this creation's resources thankfully.

We still have help when evil grips us and demands,
to raise a ruckus in God's holy sanctuary,
there is a freeing which empowers us once again.
We invite with welcome all sorts and kind of humanity.

We, too, have been saved that we might also serve
the Christ who comes into our humble homes.
There he has compassion for our present fevers.
Ours is a ministry of witness to take into the world.

A hole-patched Capernaum roof reminded many who saw
one paralyzed with guilt and near bitterness of life,
whom friends willingly transported on invalid's stretcher.
We, too, must give up fault-finding and celebrate healing.

When rough seas and wild storms rage about us,
there is one who can speak the word of blessed calm
to still the turmoils which often so threaten us.
Yet, best of all, guide us through while winds rage on.

Jesus had compassion on the many hungry listeners,
and taught the wary disciples an unforgettable lesson,
of response to need and how little becomes so much.
At his prompting they all participated in new sharing.

Blind Bartimaeus was rewarded for faith and persistence
and was given sight to follow the Christ in discipleship;
while we still puzzle why some are healed and others not.
We also learn God would not have us suffer on purpose.

The stench of death surrounded Christ's sorrow crying,
with sisters' disappointment in him very moving,
from the dead Lazarus and new life requisitioned.
Our call comes to exit the dark caves which entomb us.

The loving concern of a Gentile Centurion's ill servant
is a model of how God would have us treat each other.
This great faith was rewarded with healing at a distance.
In joy we must share our wealth and love across the races.

At Nain's east gate a widow grieves her only son;
Jesus responded as Elijah had years before him,
demonstrating his great power over death and grave.
Modeled for us disciples a ministry of compassion.

To the bent-over crippled in the spirit on a Sabbath,
Jesus gave the gift of upright posture restored.
In him is a wonderful freedom for people over laws.
Here is a warning lest we crave power instead of mercy.

So even yet today we celebrate the marvelous acts of God,
and how Jesus modeled for us discipleship of compassion,
from Centurion's little daughter to blind beggar Bartimaeus.
Life transformed to miraculous grace and profound appreciation.

Introduction

William Barclay in his helpful book on miracles titled, *And He Had Compassion*, defines these events this way: "A miracle is an event in which the power of God is brought to bear on some human situation. But a miracle in the New Testament sense is not only a wonderful work of power; it is an event which allows us to see something of God's attitude of love towards people."[1]

So here we have recorded miracles of Jesus which bring the power of God up close and personal, rearranging the person's situation. They reveal in a marvelous way God's attitude of love toward us. They had needs and Jesus had the power which no one else had.

I don't believe Jesus came with a mission to do miracles. Rather, because he had the God-power to do so, in compassion he reached out and helped. These acts always tell us something about God and also about ourselves.

My own evolution in proclaiming these stories began with a rather naive "magic of Jesus" approach. I then moved to a time when I was sure they all could be explained naturally. From there I progressed to looking mostly at what and why the Gospels wanted them told and re-told. Now I have moved to a still different approach. While considering the traditional teaching of the miracle again, I have begun to discover a "flip side." Like the old 33-1/3-rpm or 45-rpm records, there was, in addition to the main and popular side, another side often with melodies much less familiar and secondary to the main ones. But on occasion these flip sides would catch on and hit it big. So I have searched for these and given them focus in the following sermons.

One of the more far-out and radical examples would be in the sermon "Sinking Boats And Water Walking" about Jesus and Peter walking on (or through) the water that moonlit night. The traditional emphasis is made, which we have heard for years, that when we disciples are in trouble, Jesus sees it and comes to help. Then we move to a new idea about Peter jumping out of the boat. Perhaps he got out to *help* Jesus steady the little craft. And that says a lot about a role we might also assume in our discipleship. This sermon, as most contained in this book, is in a narrative form of preaching which I believe is called for by the very attractiveness and mystery of the stories.

My simple formula for presenting the miracles in narrative form goes like this:

1. Tell the story in your own words.
2. Tell what it teaches us about God.
3. Explain what it reveals about us.
4. Prayerfully discover why the author wanted this preserved.
5. Look for a fresh flip side focus.
6. Answer the "so what?" (What do we do about it?)
7. Frame by returning to the first few sentences.

I've put numbers in the sermon about Jairus' daughter and the woman with a hemorrhage corresponding to the above numbered sermon outline. If you are not given to homiletic formulas, at least consider these questions which ought to be asked in preparing to preach on these subjects:

1. What is the traditional theme?
2. Why did the writer want this told and what did it illustrate in early preaching?
3. What does the story tell us about God and us humans?
4. Can I find a fresh approach (a flip side) which may be a second-ary focus?
5. So what must I do this week in response to this miracle lesson?

Read on that you might be moved to marvel with me at God's love for us. And please help yourself to any of my simple thoughts for your preaching. Perhaps there in the pulpit yet more miracles of God's power and presence will take place.

— JLS

---

1. William Barclay, *And He Had Compassion* (Edinburg: St. Andrew Press, 1975), p. 6.

A Congregational President And His Sick Daughter

Matthew 9:18-26

Death flutes wailed a morbid tune for Jairus' daughter;
at life's end our graceful God provides for us and loved ones,
By touch old woman's hemorrhage dried from compassion,
Even when ridiculed, health and wellness is our ministry.

(1)If Matthew were to have told the tale in contemporary language of our day, he might have said it like this: While Jesus was holding an evangelism rally in a local church, the president of the congregation told him he just got a call that his twelve-year-old daughter had suddenly died. Shaken and unsteady, he asked if Jesus would come home with him and place his hand on her little body, praying she would have eternal life. They quickly headed for the subway station to go to the home of the little girl. In the crowd at the station someone touched Jesus' coat. The president of the congregation, named Jairus, was impatient and wanted to quickly dismiss this encounter with a wretched homeless woman, who had had a problem of uterine bleeding for years now and was always hanging around there. She had gone to many of the city's clinics, but no one seemed to help. Her health insurance had run out. In spite of the protest of Jairus, Jesus turned to this poor woman and assured her that because of her faith she was healed. They then went on to Jairus' house in the suburbs where the neighbors had gathered, the coroner had been called, and the local funeral director awaited his verdict. It was a hysterical atmosphere! Neighbor kids were crying, friends of Jairus' wife had gathered in the bedroom, and one set of grandparents just couldn't be comforted. The brother of the little girl played his CD with high volume. Jesus asked them to step out of the bedroom and he and three of his theological students went up to the bed.

Checking for a pulse in the main artery of the neck, he discovered she was not dead but in a coma or insulin shock. He told her to get up ... and she did! He instructed others to feed her right away. All through the neighborhood the story was told that day about a misdiagnosis and new life for a precious little girl just down the block by a visiting evangelist.

It was a marvelous day in Jesus' life when he gave new life and a different life to two people. (2)It certainly shows us some beautiful things about our God we have gathered to worship today. Even though Jairus was a leader in the synagogue and would probably have hated Jesus and the new thinking he proclaimed, Jesus still felt sorry for a father whose daughter was dying.

God is like that. God loves us in spite of our weak faith or poor attitude. We can come to a God like this no matter how disreputable we have been in the past. We can come to a God like this and request our miracles without fear that God will ignore us because of our past sins or lack of faithfulness to Christ's Church. There will be no checking of our communion or contribution record. Our God does not want to be our judge, according to John, but rather our Savior (John 3:17). God still wants to help in spite of all our poor motivations. So we can put it bluntly: We have a very graceful God.

John Newton wrote it this way: "Through many dangers, toils, and snares, I have already come; 'Tis grace has brought me safe thus far, and grace will lead me home." Amazing Grace, how sweet the sound!

By far the main teaching about God here in these two stories is that we have a profound comfort not only in lengthy suffering, but in death itself. Since these events, Jesus has gone to the cross for our forgiveness and come out of Jerusalem's Easter grave so we also can say of our loved ones — "They are asleep." Death is not the end. We have a life with this Christ beyond the earthly grave or cremation. It is in Christ and thus we sleep and move into a new relationship with our God.

At the funeral home or church sanctuaries, we have a profound presence of the Christ who assures us our loved ones are okay. They are asleep. Perhaps we need to review again what those of faith, our church foremothers and fathers, knew and wrote down for us: "I believe in the resurrection of the body and life everlasting." They are asleep. We who remain a while longer are comforted. And we have courage to face an uncertain future unafraid. Any Christ who would go to such individual trouble as this one in going to the home of a man who probably opposed him, and healing his daughter; any Christ who would stop on the way and help a woman who managed to touch him in the crowd, will certainly help us when we ask it also.

(3)We learn a lot about ourselves in these experiences as well. Although our motivation is for the wrong reason and our faith inadequate, and we are one in many who have needs, the Christ will still help. I surely like this idea of the importance of the individual in our religion. For we live in a day of big numbers and mass communication, and often sacrificing the individual "for the good of the many." Here, just the touch of the fringe of Jesus' robe was noticed. And he stopped to see who had needed his attention. In the midst of that large pressing crowd and the hurry to get to Jairus' home, he stopped, and that one wretched woman had his complete, undivided attention. Wonderful! I'll bet he notices us in the same individual way, too. You know he could have said to Jairus, "I can't leave all these people here in the synagogue right now. I must stay here and continue to teach. But instead, for one little girl in one little Palestinian home, he went home with Jairus. That's really hope-filled for us. We count, we are important, we are very precious to none other than the creator of the whole universe. We are more than our social security and credit card numbers. We are God's individual daughters and sons.

In 1994 during the bloody civil and tribal war in Liberia, I visited a displaced-person camp in a swampy area, called Brewersville, in order to take some rice to a mother and children we knew. The horrid conditions were beyond description. One elder came into the Lutheran World Relief medical tent carrying a dead little child. He explained that about one a day dies there. I recall

17

walking between the little mud huts with the hungry people pulling at my clothing, begging for money or food. It must have been like that for Jesus that day as he made his way with Jairus toward his home.

This story within a story, of Jesus stopping to heal the outcast woman who had hemorrhaged for years, tells us today we ought to give similar attention to the marginalized in our own day and culture. There are always those people who are not "our people," who just don't fit in with the majority, who don't dress or behave like the rest of us who need our attention. The church often attracts such as these, as it should, because it's one of the very few places where some will try their best to love and accept them. Because this woman had a continued loss of blood from the genital area for all these years, she was considered "unclean" and probably was even physically unclean in that day of much less sanitary supplies to help cope with the problem. So she was forbidden in church, to touch anyone else, or even be around where they lived.

We must be sure we see those of our day who are considered by our society as unclean. We must love them on God's behalf. You can draw up the list. Some are more acceptable than others: those with AIDS; the mentally and physically challenged; the so-called "street people"; those of skin color different than ours; and the people of different sexual preferences than the majority. All these we must welcome and encourage into our loving fellowship.

I hope Jairus, after this woman's illness was healed, invited her to church next Sabbath with his alive daughter and family! I hope she was welcomed there with great enthusiasm.

Speaking of Jairus, how about Jesus going home with him? Doesn't this tell us Jesus wants to go home with us also? I think so. Our tendency is to think of being with Jesus here in church and somehow separate him from our home life and family. Here we learn we can and ought to take him home. It's one thing to be loving and gentle and kind here in the church building, but quite something else to take that behavior home and practice it there all week. He can work miracles there still. Pettiness can be changed into an attitude of generosity, hostility into loving concern, getting even into undeserved forgiveness.

18

It's obvious that we have the kind of Savior who wants to bring peace and healing into our homes. This Savior is eager to bless where we live with an aura of kindness toward each other. This Savior likes to heal the hurts and pain we have brought to each other. This Christ wants to help us be faithful to our marriage covenant of fidelity and restore deep love between husband and wife, parents and children, family and neighbors.

This same Jesus, when we take him home with us, wants our homes to be places of warm hospitality and welcome to others, like orphans and refugees, abandoned and abused. The old and lonely, the young and rebellious, ought to find comfort and security there.

That same home with Jesus present can be a place of frequent prayer before meals and at bedtime. It can be where the Bible is read and discussed and where witness is taught and taken out into our daily lives.

(4)It's always important to consider why the writer of the Gospel, in this case Matthew, wanted this story told and preserved. Matthew always writes his accounts in order to instruct. This Gospel is sometimes called the "teaching Gospel." Here he wanted to instruct us about the power of the Savior. There are three miracle stories grouped together by Matthew which demonstrate God had power over evil, sickness, and even death. No doubt these were to prove to the people who heard them what it can be like when the kingdom of God breaks into our daily life. It turns the world, as we know it, upside down. It brings unity where there has been such strife. The kingdom helps us live with each other knowing we are not perfect, but that we are forgiven. So Matthew told the stories to let us know the power of God in bringing the kingdom into our world and lives. Thanks, Matt, we needed that!

(5)The flip side (or other side) of these two brief stories of healing would ask us to *consider ministries which bring Jesus out of our churches and into our homes.* I think, especially in light of the healings, of the possibilities and needs of our people for a ministry of health and wholeness taken from our churches out into our homes. Oh, the things a Christian nurse can accomplish when she or he goes into the homes of the elderly, the confused, the ill, the lonely, whom HMOs and other schemes of health care will not serve.

As our health care has gotten more and more impersonal, we disciples need to step in and minister to the individual woman the crowd ignores and the daughter the father was so worried about. With children and youth in general, we have something to offer. We can bring Jesus to touch them with his loving concern in homes where parents have gotten trapped into being far too busy and distracted to do good parenting.

There may be something else here. When Jesus said of Jairus' daughter, "The girl is not dead, but asleep," Matthew said, "But they laughed at him" (Matthew 9:24). Ridicule is hard to take for your belief. It did not deter Jesus. He continued his act of mercy. When we are ridiculed, perhaps we should do the same. It doesn't help to argue or prove you are right. It doesn't help to get others to join on your side. Just continue your discipleship and let your humble service and the results of it be the witness to how God can change things in our lives and our outlook on life. I don't think anyone has ever been argued into the kingdom. But many, many, upon seeing devoted, humble service for, and to, the Master, have found their cynical attitude removed and the faith of the believer become gradually attractive as a way of life for them. I'll bet those who laughed at Jesus that day had some second thoughts when that little daughter of Jairus came out of the bedroom to go to the kitchen for some food. I'll guess, too, that Jesus had to remind the disciples not to take an attitude of "I told you so," but rather to continue on with their ministry of compassion. After all, changed lives are still the most persuasive and convincing way to prove Jesus is real, and we have a powerful God who loves us.

(6)Let's continue our service this week even though some laugh. Let's explore ways we can more fully develop a health ministry from our congregation. Let's all take Jesus home with us today. Let's be comforted no matter how small we think we are. Jesus sees us and cares. Let's be on guard for the outsiders in our midst so that we can involve them. And when death comes to our loved one, let us be lifted up and encouraged with the promise of life beyond the grave.

(7)In contemporary language we might complete the story like this: That evening at the big evangelism rally at the church, there were some new faces in the pews. There was an older woman who had never felt welcome there who sang the song, "Amazing Grace," with an off-tone gusto, nearly shouting the words, "... who saved a wretch like me." She had been brought by the president of the congregation and sat next to a little twelve-year-old girl who seemed extra vibrant and alive, whose neighbors were seated toward the back. About all these new-found worshipers, the rest of that congregation just weren't quite sure.

Note: The numbers in parentheses indicate the seven points of the sermon development. See the introduction for clarification.

Sinking Boats
And Water Walking

Matthew 14:22-33

Don't be afraid, the first thought apparition spoke,
Across the turbulent waves and strong Galilee wind,
For in the ship of church we are secure with Savior,
And, like Peter, must willingly jump in to offer assist.

It was early February and because of severe flooding of the San Francisco delta, there were many plastic bags which had been used for sand bags floating in the Sacramento River. One of those empty bags got into our boat engine's intake for cooling and plugged it. In no time, the motor overheated and began to burn the rubber hoses, etc., causing heavy smoke to come from the stern. To the starboard was nothing but sand hills and wind-powered electric generators. To the port, tules and peat forming Winter Island. There was no possible help in sight. My wife put on her life jacket and climbed out onto the bow ready to abandon ship in case of explosion. I put down an anchor to prevent the current from banging us against the distant shore and put in a frantic "mayday" call to the Rio Vista U.S. Coast Guard. "Mayday, mayday, we are on fire and need immediate assistance."

The young radio operator responded with question after question, but no immediate help. "Skipper, do you have your life jacket on? Have you put down an anchor? What is your CF number? Tell me your location." I answered them all and asked, "Have you dispatched any help for us yet? We are on fire!" The answer came back, "What is your location again?" I replied, "Just tell me, is the Coast Guard on the way ..." The reply was so disheartening, I could imagine the cold water of that river in February. "No, skipper, we don't have any craft to send to your aid. Tell me again your registration number. How large are the flames now?" I began to think — just how was it that Jesus walked on water? And what mistake had Peter made which caused him to sink? Thank God it's daytime!

Then, over the radio came a deep strong voice which sounded like God's ought to sound. He said, "This is 'Vessel Assist' and we are on our way. Watch up river to your starboard and you'll see our signal from a mirror in the sunlight." We did see it soon. They came alongside. By then the burning of the rubber connections to the engine had slowed considerably. They threw us a line, we weighed anchor and were towed four or five nautical miles into the Pittsburg marina where a credit card had to be produced for the rescue.

It wasn't quite like that on Galilee lake's north end. According to Matthew's account, after the feeding of the large crowd, there was an excited effort to make Jesus king, so he sent the disciples in their boat back home toward their base of operations, Capernaum. It was his plan to go alone up the mountainside for rest and prayer, away from them all. It didn't go well in their boat either. Nothing caught fire, but the wind came up strongly and blew against the direction they were trying to go. And the waves slammed against the bow to prevent them from making progress. About three in the morning, they had been blown dangerously close to shore and shallow sandbars. From his vantage point with a full moon, Jesus could see their struggle and came out to the rescue. First, they thought he was a ghost; then, when he called to them, "Take courage! It is I. Don't be afraid," (Matthew 14:27) they knew who it was. From a previous storm in that same boat they also knew they were now safe. Sure enough, "And when they (Jesus and Peter) climbed into the boat, the wind died down" (Matthew 14:32).

There have been many attempts to explain this story. Basically there are two ways of looking at it. Both are plausible and valid. The first would be to say here was another work of the miracles by Jesus who has the power to do that sort of thing. He literally walked on water. The second would be, which the original language sup-

24

ports also, that he came out through the surf on the shallow sand-bar to help manage the boat. It looked like he was on top of the water that moonlit night.

Either way you explain it, *the real message for us is that when the disciples were in trouble, Jesus came and helped.* That night he was the "vessel rescue" of Galilee's lake.

I lean toward the second explanation because I find it more promising for me when I'm in trouble. In my storms, when the winds blow the opposite way I must go and the waves are frighten-ing, I'd rather count on a Christ who would come to help me through the storm than ask Christ to work a miracle to stop the storm.

The story says to me that we do not struggle alone. The very God who called this universe into being and keeps it running now comes to us when we have need. That God probably doesn't still the storm, but that God sees us through it. Like California's Vessel Assist, Jesus throws us a line, gets in the boat with us, and brings us safely to shore. That was so much a part of Matthew, Mark, and John's experience in their struggles, that all three wrote it down for us to hear and read today!

Traditionally, over the years, the boat in this storm has repre-sented the church. It's a symbol still maintained in many places. When we look at it this way we see that Christians for two thou-sand years have taken comfort in knowing that even in the wildest storms the world can deal out to us, we can ride them out in our boat, the church of Jesus Christ. The seas have rarely been calm for the church. The power that works against God continues to blow contrary wind and stirs up the waves against us. It looks to me like there are even heavier seas ahead as the secular world be-comes increasingly hostile toward our church. The red flags of navigation warning are up and we're in for a rough ride, just like those disciples long ago and far away from here.

But, we must remember in our struggle against the world's havoc and attempts to capsize and sink us — we are not alone. Jesus sees our plight from the shore and still comes to help. He has gone to the cross for our forgiveness; he has come out of the grave so we might also come out of the grave, and he has returned in spirit to equip us for times just like these.

In our culture and country, the most treacherous storm might be a deadly calm when spiritual lives are neglected and the young are given an indirect message that it's not all that significant. There is an undercurrent which says we're now smarter and the church just isn't important any longer.

Worst of all may be the way we allow pursuits of a false happiness, like getting things and accumulating more and more wealth, to crowd our lives from discipleship. The boat of the church is all the time taking on more and more of the sea while we blithely go about our self-centered existence.

There are many things which threaten to swamp our boat: church quarrels, struggles over power in the congregation and in our national church bodies. The way we sometimes attack each other denominationally may be causing black smoke to come from the stern as well. It smells and it is an ugly sight which repels many.

Those are the traditional ways preachers have looked at this marvelous story of storm and moonlight and fear of ghosts on Galilee. Now let's turn the story around a bit and see what its flip side might be for us today.

Knowing Peter's personality a little from studying the Bible, perhaps he was trying to help when he came out of the boat to Jesus on the water. The scripture says: "Then Peter got down out of the boat, walked on the water and came toward Jesus. But when he saw the wind, he was afraid and, beginning to sink, cried out, 'Lord, save me!' " (Matthew 14:29-30). As a lifelong boater, I can see it happening. How many of us in rough water have jumped for dock or shore to secure the line to a cleat only to miss and get soaking wet? Peter was that kind of disciple. His boat was out of control! Jesus was coming to help moor and steady it. He couldn't do it by himself. They were heading toward him too fast! So out of the bow he jumped into the water of that familiar landing place close to his mother-in-law's house. Then in the confusion of wind, darkness, strong waves, and a moving boat, he mis-stepped and sank. Jesus grabbed him and lifted him up again.

That's a little different than the way it's portrayed in stained glass in our churches, but I like the concept because it helps us, on this flip side of the miracle, to talk about our role as disciples helping Jesus today.

Peter had shouted to Jesus, "...'tell me to come to you on the water.' 'Come,' he said" (Matthew 14:28-29). There is something about Peter to admire. While he often put his foot in his mouth when he spoke, while he acted before he thought and was brash and crude, there was a wonderful quality of wanting to help Jesus. The rest of the disciples played it safe and probably never even thought of jumping in to help. Good old impulsive Peter jumped in. What a leap it was! First over his head and then the strong hand of the Savior lifted him up. He told of it often in his preaching the rest of his ministry.

I believe God calls us out of the boat to help also. And sometimes we have a sinking feeling we should not have acted so impulsively. We would have been better off to ask a lot more questions, like the radio operator of the Rio Vista station when I called in an urgent "Mayday!"

Ask yourself in the calm of the seas here in our congregation, "What is Jesus asking me to do to help?"

— Should I be preparing to be an ordained pastor?
— Have I learned enough Bible to be an effective disciple?
— Is a tithe enough for me in the weekly offering?
— Given my skills, gifts, and abilities, what is the ministry Jesus calls me to do all week long?
— Am I doing the best possible parenting in these stormy times for youth?
— How can I make a difference in our congregational life here so we can be a "vessel rescue" for others in mighty storms in our neighborhood?
— Am I as effective and bold as I should be in witness and inviting others to be in this same boat with me called the church?

The rest of the disciples in the boat stayed there and fretted about the waves and head wind and questioned whether Jesus could do anything about it. Peter jumped in and offered to help. Is it too much to imagine Peter then saying to Jesus, "Okay, I got the bow; you grab the stern"?

The Church of Jesus Christ is always in need of volunteers who can feel in their hearts what ought to be done and jump in to try. We often go at it all wrong; we sometimes make it worse; we sometimes nearly drown others in the process. But if you consider all the rapids, the height of the waves, velocity of the wind, and sea-worthiness of the boat, you may never get started to help, much like that Rio Vista Coast Guard radio operator. This sermon may be Jesus' way of saying to you, "Come," just as he did to that impulsive, big-hearted fisherman, Peter.

"Come," Jesus says when we are asked:
— to serve on the church governing board;
— to be a visitor for evangelism or stewardship;
— to be a church school teacher;
— to help with the youth ministry program;
— to sing in the choir, or serve on the altar guild;
— to visit the homebound with the sacrament;
— to lead a Bible study or help maintain the property.

All these are always in need of disciples and sailors who will jump in with Peter and help none other than Jesus.

The church is a great boat ride over seas calm and turbulent. We are in this boat together as disciples. *In this story, we have an assurance that we can get through no matter how rough the storm because we are not alone.* No matter how you explain that middle of the night miracle, there is great comfort and instruction in it.

Since our terrifying boating experience on the Delta's Sacramento River, we've joined the organization "Vessel Assist" which is like a "AAA" for boaters. It's comforting to know they are ready to help in any emergency.

Peter was ready to help. Jesus saw the problem and did help those disciples. He'll help us too.

28

One Out Of Ten Isn't All That Bad

Luke 17:11-19

The fulfilled life of discipleship is constant gratitude,
knowing the marvelous grace-gift God has tendered
to heal us of our maladies and natural sinfulness.
We are to care for this creation's resources thankfully.

Tom Brokaw, on the NBC evening news on Thanksgiving eve, said, "When we sing the dirges, we must also sing the anthem." He went on to say we must "... recognize not only the miseries of life but also the joys." So it is being a sinner and living in an imperfect world.

Our Gospel story makes a similar point. Luke, who often writes about healings because of his medical expertise, emphasizes a favorite theme of his: the universality of God's salvation and the consideration of Samaritans as God's people.

You know the story well by now. We usually read it on Thanksgiving. Jesus was on his way to Jerusalem where he would go to the cross for our forgiveness. Ten lepers, at the edge of a little town where they were forced to live because of that malady, shouted out a request that he cure them. Jesus told them to go to their priest, a common way Jews were proven cleared of their skin disease and pronounced safe to re-enter into the life of the community again. On their way to do so, they were cured.

One returned to find Jesus and thank him. The one who returned was not a Jew as you might expect, but was a person the Jews thought of as pagan — he was a Samaritan who was the son of a Jew marrying a Gentile. Jesus showed disappointment that the others did not return to show their appreciation as well. He commended the Samaritan for his faith and sent him on his way.

Leprosy was a horrible disease. Not only were the dreadful physical symptoms slowly rotting away their bodies, but also the wretched way they were marginalized and treated by the community was devastating. I saw it several places in the world. We Christians have two leper colonies in Liberia, West Africa, called "Ganta" and "Little Ganta," located on the only "coal-tar road" going north and south in the country. I believe it was the Methodists who have led the way in a very compassionate ministry there. The disfigurement of the residents is difficult to observe, but everything is done to bring the compassion and healing of Christ to them.

Weekly Jesus works again the miracle of making them clean of the dreaded skin diseases with the use of up-to-date medications and therapy. They are healed and they thank God in their little chapel over and over again.

Near the village of Zorzor, south of Ganta, is "Little Ganta." Here the science is not yet as advanced. The facilities are a safe distance from Zorzor and the thatched roof, mud-sided huts are much more primitive. Those who live there are the products of earlier days when leprosy was without hope of a cure. It is a pitiful sight. Yet, in their affliction, they came together to thank God they have each other.

Perhaps that's the first thing we ought to look at today. In Luke's story we notice that these ten outcasts were a mixture of Jew and Gentile (Samaritan). Isn't it interesting how adversity can draw us closer to each other? An earthquake, hurricane, fire, flood, or war seems to cause us to reach across those many barriers which otherwise, in good times, separate us. Perhaps that's one of the blessings God can give to us when we are devastated by the traumatic events of our lives. Those barriers of race or creed or class or ethnic origin or sexual preference, which we artificially and demonically erect, God erases when we no longer have the luxury to observe them.

It's not the major teaching of this miracle of healing, but it does say loudly to us to rid ourselves of those perverse prejudices and hatreds we somehow learn over the years. That is not the way

God would have us see each other. Like those lepers, we are all in need of God's mercy and salvation. That should bring us together as one people who cry out in one voice, "Jesus, Master, have pity on us!" (Luke 17:13b).

Here is really the heart of this story: Ten were given health and new life and only one of them returned to express gratitude to Jesus. I'm sure Jesus wasn't disappointed that day because he didn't receive more praise, but rather, that those nine didn't begin a new kind of life of appreciation like the Samaritan. It was nice for the one thanked, but much more so for the one who did the thanking. They were new people with a different perspective on life and God's role in it. He wanted that for them to go along with their starting over as clean and healthy. But it was not to be.

When the Israelites came into the promised land after that very long time in the wilderness, God warned them of the danger of ingratitude: "When you have eaten and are satisfied, praise the Lord your God for the good land he has given you. Be careful that you do not forget the Lord your God ..." (Deuteronomy 8:10-11a).

When I voice disappointment in my children, grandchildren, or close friends for whom I have done something nice, my wife will say, "Jerry, you shouldn't have done it expecting to be thanked." She's right. But I so want those I love to know the richness of a life of thankfulness. It's the crown and completion of our faith. To live in that kind of graceful attitude is to face life's problems and frustrations in a very different way. It's really God's special equipment for us to receive as a gift as well. I want that blessing for all of us and Jesus wanted it so much for all ten he had healed.

"Were not all ten cleansed? Where are the other nine?" (Luke 17:17). Here is disappointment that the nine would not know the joy of a life of gratitude like the one. Their faith would remain puny, to be a backup in times of life's serious crises rather than faith permeating all of life with a wonderfully resilient joy of appreciation.

I wonder if this miracle doesn't prod us to examine our lives and seek out those who have shaped, loved, and cared for us for a new word of thanksgiving. I think of a sainted mother, a loving pastor, several inspirational school teachers, several devoted professors, and a late college and seminary classmate to whom this little volume is dedicated. Of course, my gentle wife who in many cases loves me "anyhow" would be in the first of those to whom I owe so much. And then there are our many children and grandchildren who now enrich our lives in ways we never expected.

Let this sermon cause you to take inventory also — and then express your appreciation to those you can before the sun goes down on this day. Don't be an "other-niner" (not to be confused with my Forty-niners) — be a returning Samaritan at the feet of the one who saved us, giving thanks.

There is a flip side to this story of one-out-of-nine that I believe is worth exploring with you. I doubt this side is considered very often, but it is crucial to our practice of the faith here in North America. This flip side has to do with *keeping our distance from Jesus, our ingratitude for the world around us, and our mission and ministry to bring healing to the lepers of our day.*

Especially during my years of parish ministry, I noticed that many Christians and members of the church, while occasionally coming to worship, were like those ten who needed healing. "They stood at a distance" (Luke 17:12b). While we can be members, attend almost regularly, give in the offering, and even serve in some way like ushering or singing in the choir, all of that can be at a safe distance. We do that which is the minimum required in our culture to be considered a Christian and member of a church. But there is a distance between us and Jesus. Our loyalty may be to the congregation, but not to the Christ.

There is a deeper spirituality available to us which calls for moving with that healed Samaritan from standing at a distance to throwing ourselves at Jesus' feet and thanking him. I believe many congregations even level out any tendency of the new Christian to give themselves in a wholehearted fashion to the Christ. We subtly advise not to be "too radical" about our newfound joy lest we embarrass those who live their faith at a bit of a distance. In our worship of God, our ministry in daily life, and especially in our witness to others about the gospel, we often indicate to the more "gung-ho" and enthusiastic not to "go overboard." And so we shape another of the nine who remain into rather bland but socially-acceptable Christians. Jesus commended this one Samaritan because his thankfulness was unrestrained. There ought to be times like that for us, too.

It's probably stretching a lot what Luke wanted said about this parable, but I still want to do it here on the flip side. A life of appreciation for the Eden in which we have been given to live means a life of careful stewardship of our environment and natural resources. To appreciate our good place to live is to thank God by conserving it gently for future generations. To appreciate our comfortable surroundings is to love and minister to that non-human world, considering it as the beaten-up traveler along Jericho's roadway in need of help, just like another Samaritan did whom Luke also told us about.

Just as we talk about child abuse and sexual abuse, there is also resource abuse. God has given us a wonderful, good lifestyle with enough natural resources to live comfortably. We must be good stewards of those resources in order that future generations might also share them. The percentage, in my judgment, is still about one out of ten who respond appropriately to the gifts of creation. Certainly a congregation has the responsibility to conduct its affairs with a careful eye toward the stewardship of resources. Not only should we be careful how much offering money we spend on ourselves, but also how much electricity, natural gas, paper, or gasoline we expend as our share of what God provides. To be thankful is to be a good steward in all areas of our lives.

In our education ministry, as thankful people, we must instruct our young to be appropriately thankful by practicing this kind of ecological stewardship. In fact, our young probably have a keener sense of this responsibility than our older, already-set-in-our-ways generation.

On the flip side of this story of ingratitude is a mandate for us. Because Jesus did this healing on his way to Jerusalem, and because he still tried to work the miracle within the framework of the church, it seems to me this is still one of our ministry tasks on God's behalf within our congregation. It's a ministry of health and wholeness that thankfulness and God's love can provide. Jesus evidently thought it important and something we should do. (I doubt it was so we would have a message for our American holiday of Thanksgiving.)

33

There is still so much healing to be done in our time. Those whose minds are distorted by hate, those whose lives are paralyzed by guilt, those who have become totally possessed by an addiction, those who suffer with depression or lack of self-worth — there are many who stand at our village gate and cry out, "Master, have pity on us!" (Luke 17:13b). We can help. We can make a dramatic difference in their lives with the love of Christ through us to them. And we can provide a ministry to the old who fear being alone and the young who fear new relationships, with great measures of Jesus' healing love given through us. It's our mission, too.

Not all will return to give thanks. In fact, the percentage might be about one-in-ten here also. However, we take our model from Jesus and the lepers of his day. We continue our ministry of compassion anyway.

So this flip side challenge is for a ministry of healing, the care of natural resources, and living a spiritual life much closer to Jesus. Tom Brokaw of the NBC *Nightly News* was correct, "When we sing the dirges, we must also sing the anthem. We recognize not only the miseries of life but also the joys." We ought to take inventory and thank those who have done so much. An attitude of appreciation is a part of the Christian life and, oh how often the blessing of a disaster is the breaking down of the barriers we have erected to divide us.

May Jesus say to us today, "Rise and go; your faith has made you well" (Luke 17:19).

When Demons
Come To Church

Mark 1:21-28

---

*We still have help when evil grips us and demands
to raise a ruckus in God's holy sanctuary,
there is a freeing which empowers us once again.
We invite with welcome all sorts and kinds of humanity.*

In my younger years this was not such a difficult miracle of Jesus to explain. But now, after many years of ministry and experiences of unexplained demonic situations and people, I'm not all that sure.

It's probably from some writing named "A day in Capernaum." According to Mark's account, Jesus had been announced by his cousin, John the Baptist, then baptized by him. He chose his ministry style by being tempted in the wilderness; and after calling his first disciples, it was time to begin. They started out with a bang in the synagogue at Capernaum. Jesus was the guest teacher that Sabbath. It was going very well because, unlike the teachers who quoted others for their authority, he spoke with his own authority and belief. This amazed his listeners.

Then it happened! A man there started to raise a ruckus. Mark and Luke, who probably heard Peter tell about that very day, said the man "... who was possessed by an evil spirit cried out ..." (Mark 1:23), not the last person to cause a disturbance in church, I dare say!

Demon possession was an accepted belief of those ancient times. Scholars still find in graveyards skulls which have had a hole cut in them to let the evil spirits out. It was thought by most that two angels named Assael and Shemachsai revolted against God because of their lust for mortal women and produced children which became the world's demons. This was so firmly believed that by the year 340 A.D. the Christian church had an order of exorcism.

One hundred years ago, preachers simply told of this incident in the Capernaum synagogue with a sense of awe at the marvelous power of this Messiah Jesus. They claimed it was the beginning of a new ministry by "the Holy One of God" (Mark 1:24b). And there was a wonderful air about the telling we would describe today as, "Hang on to your hats, folks, this Savior and his days on earth are going to be something awesome."

Since psychological science and understanding of mental health have come into their own, we now have taken another look and would explain the demon-possessed man as a mental patient with neurotic problems. We have said also that Jesus simply helped him by accepting what the man believed about demon possession. Jesus' confident, firm, authoritative manner, using the same words he would in stilling the storm later, reassured the man, much like he would the storm in that Lake Galilee squall which so terrified the sailors.

There are times we need such calming in our lives. Jesus can do that for us. He points out a confidence that he is always with us, gives us a new set of priorities, provides friends so we are not alone, and points us to the cross to assure us we are forgiven. For our help we are provided medication, therapy, and support groups to see us through.

The demonic is still with us and after us, although we have given it various clinical names. Oh, we don't talk any longer about a personal devil in long red underwear, with tail, horns, and a pitch-fork. Still, we can be consumed (possessed) by powers which rule our lives, like alcoholism, wealth addiction, racism which per-verts creation itself, sexual obsession and abuse, drug addiction, lust for power, and plain old guilt, greed, and self-centeredness called narcissism.

This miracle does tell us there is a power greater than these. To be in Christ gives us a spirit and others to help us break free, overcome, and regain mental health.

I'm really glad for this story of healing in the Capernaum synagogue, for it reassures me that our Christ is interested in our mental and physical health as well as the security in eternity of our soul. No wonder Saint Luke, the doctor, also told this story, probably with great delight.

Mental health professionals perhaps say a quiet, "Hallelujah!" at its reading, for it affirms a certain Christ-like ministry to those whose mental faculties have become, for whatever reason, disoriented. And it argues strongly for Christian mental health and medical institutions and chaplains. There is a wholeness about the Christian in mind, spirit, and body.

On the flip side of this exorcism in the Capernaum synagogue is a little detail important for us who are members of congregations. *When this demon-possessed man caused a disturbance in worship, Jesus did not have him removed from among the listeners.*

Because the Christian church does and should attract all sorts of people, from misfits to malcontents to egomaniacs, there will always be those who cause a ruckus in the congregation. The demonic has put on church clothes and has joined us for worship, often affecting our imperfect attempt at ministry. It's clear from this story we should not only encourage them to be there with all their unpleasantness, peculiar behavior, and downright strangeness, but we should reach out to them with God's undeserved and forgiving, graceful love that healing might take place. And even if it does not take place, where is a better place for them to be than in our congregation of believers and forgiven saints?

The flip side of this miracle of driving out an evil spirit is also this: Instead of explaining the event as something we can now put in psychological terms as to why the man behaved as he did and how Jesus dealt with it as sort of a supernatural psychiatrist, let's consider *the real possibility that there is still a strong demonic power which works against God!* — And that so far medical science has not been able to discover a physical power to overcome it.

As a young pastor I was sure I could rationalize away this act of exorcism by Jesus in the church that day in Capernaum. Like some other miracles, it could also be rationally explained how Jesus did it and why it worked. We could relegate the whole matter of demon possession to the sphere of primitive thought.

I'm not so sure any longer!

My many years of ministry and travels to many cultures have caused me to take another look. I believe the other side of this miracle is the demonic's presence yet today in an unexplainable way in our world, even with all its sophistication and diagnosis. There is still a very strong, addictive power, well-organized, which works against God and God's church and ministries. While it is obvious in other lands, it is also here with us.

I witnessed it in Liberia, West Africa, as I was preaching through an interpreter into the Loma language. Wozi, in the interior, is a center of animism. They had laid a vine around the entire town to keep me out. During my preaching the "Lion" came to town to try to scare my young listeners away from hearing the gospel. They also played drums and danced outside the building to drown out the gospel proclamation. But through all the fear and superstition, we were heard and the Holy Spirit moved some to believe. Still, there is the demonic which tries to drown out the gospel in our communities.

We have not arrived at perfection yet in the field of mental and physical health science. Just as we have not yet discovered the reason or cure for cancer or AIDS, we have not yet learned the reason for the demonic which still enters us and destroys the way God would have us be.

Often the role of our faith is to cope with that which we may someday, but do not yet, understand. So, we who are Jesus' contemporary disciples in the synagogues of our towns today do have a remedy for the threat and presence of the demonic in our lives. Like this disruptive man at Capernaum, we also have a Savior here who says today: "Come out of him (or her)" (Mark 1:25b). In the confession and absolution, and in the real presence of Jesus at communion, that which is demonic and rules us can be defeated and called out.

We even have a bonus which that Capernaum fellow didn't have available yet. Through our baptism, like that of Jesus in the wilderness, we have God's powerful Holy Spirit which wants to crowd out the not-as-strong demonic one.

It's time to recognize again that there is a strong and effective power which works against God. It cannot yet be described in medical textbooks or diagnosed with a suggested medication therapy. But it's there. And so is the Christ. And he calls even today through this sermon, hymn singing, praying, confession, communing, and what Jesus did on that cross of Calvary. — Come out of him! Come out of her! Be quiet and come out! Amen.

Blessed Are
The Mothers-in-Law

Mark 1:29-39

We, too, have been saved that we might also serve
the Christ who comes into our humble homes.
There he has compassion for our present fevers.
Ours is a ministry of witness to take into the world.

If one takes a boat ride up to the north end of the Sea of Galilee, along the shore not far from the Mount of Beatitudes monastery, one will see the ruins of the synagogue at Capernaum. Only recently have biblical archeologists made a fascinating discovery nearby. As they removed the sand accumulation of many years, the circular foundation of an old church was there. And reading the inscriptions on the stone makes clear this ancient church was built over the location of Simon Peter's home.

So, it was here, after an exhausting morning of teaching in the nearby synagogue that, according to the Gospel writer Mark, Jesus amazed the people by calling demons out of a man — one of Jesus' first miracles.

What happened next is even more amazing. The disciples and Jesus walked over to the home of Peter, his wife, her mother, and his brother, Andrew. In that house, now marked by a circular church foundation, lived an old woman and her daughter, who had married a big fisherman of Galilee. His brother had convinced him to leave their fishing business and follow a strange carpenter's son from Nazareth. Finally she could meet this wise wonder worker firsthand.

41

When the little group arrived for food and rest, a high malaria fever had her in bed shivering and in no condition to serve them the meal she had promised her daughter she would prepare. It was like any grandmother who had carefully planned a Sunday dinner for her children and grandchildren only to come down with the flu early that morning. Of all the rotten times to have that malaria flare up again!

The disciples were still pumped up with the success and acceptance of the morning's experience. Jesus was exhausted and must have felt like a contemporary pastor arriving home for lunch after three worship services and teaching Sunday School. Then, the phone rings.

Three of the Gospel writers who probably heard about it from Peter's own lips relate the story with an economy of words: Matthew used 30, it took Luke just 38, and Mark only 44. His account says simply:

> *Simon's mother-in-law was in bed with a fever, and they told Jesus about her. So he went to her, took her hand and helped her up. The fever left her and she began to wait on them.* — Mark 1:30-31

I wish I knew her name. It's just like us men not even to name her! But Christian churches ought to be named after her, for that mother-in-law of Capernaum has so much to teach us today.

What the Gospel writers do tell us is with a little different emphasis from each one: Matthew seems to center the account on Jesus as the one who carried our sicknesses as Isaiah had promised. "Surely he took up our infirmities and carried our sorrows" (Isaiah 53:4a); Luke tells the healing at Peter's home emphasizing the sovereign power of Jesus who triumphs over evil and the evil one; Mark, the earliest writer of the account, makes a more simple plea — he tells of the miracle in order to picture Jesus as the one who raises human beings from sin for the sake of service.

That's how we preachers have been seeing this story for years: we are saved by God to serve. It's the proper response to all that which God has done on the cross of Calvary, at the Easter empty tomb, and in the present time when the Holy Spirit comes upon us to equip us for full life here. It's an important learning yet today. This unnamed woman was healed and "... she began to wait on them" (Mark 1:31b). How often we are in need and trouble, pray fervently for God's help, receive it, and move on, never thinking to respond to our blessing by giving ourselves to help others because we have been helped.

I recall living in a mobile home court while attending seminary in Springfield, Ohio, years ago. Our neighbor was quite poor and lived in a very small, rundown home. He had asked me to pray that he and his wife one day could have a more comfortable, long, double-wide model. One day when I came home from classes, they were backing in a beautiful new unit on his lot. I was so happy for him as he explained they had received an unexpected inheritance from a distant aunt — so the new trailer. I remarked that we should have a time that evening to thank God for this wonderful gift. He replied that wouldn't be necessary now as the mobile home was paid for free and clear!

Peter's wife's mother saw it differently. Now that the disabling fever was gone, her natural response was to get up and serve the one who had miraculously taken it away.

It's a worthwhile reminder. If and when we are blessed with healing through a medical doctor, or through prayer, or both, we ought to see the church's plea for help in its ministry in a whole new light. And more. The great gifts of conception of a child, obtaining a new job, securing a place to live, our marriage repaired and renewed, forgiveness assured, friendship established, prayers answered, and on and on the list must go. In response to all the Christ has done and is doing for us — we gladly serve.

Wouldn't a congregation made up of Peter's mother-in-laws be a great place to belong and worship!

Notice, too, something important about Jesus' ministry. He didn't need an audience to help; no grandstander was this Savior! In fact, in most instances of working a miracle he tried his best to keep the act quiet so as not to be linked to so-called magic workers of his day. It seems to me he worked his miracles mainly because he had the power to do so and was compelled to help someone who

43

needed his help. And even though he was worn out and needed rest, he was willing to help this suffering, fever-filled, old woman who was the mother of Andrew's big brother, Peter.

Now the flip side of this private, Sabbath noon Capernaum miracle. Perhaps the three Gospel writers wanted us to see that right at the start of Jesus' ministry *he took the power of church out into the home.* By telling us this intimate story of healing, I think the disciples wanted us to know Jesus blesses home and family when he is present. No difficulty is too insignificant at home to bring to Jesus. No struggle is outside his ability to make better or solve, or heal.

Notice on this flip side of the miracle that it's one thing to go to church and witness marvelous changes take place in those assembled. It's another thing to take that Spirit of God home with us and bless our marriage, our parenting, our stewardship of family with it.

I've always been glad for this little story because it shows Peter was married — you can't get a mother-in-law any other way, even in Capernaum! Sometimes we forget this big part of the disciples' lives. Peter had a wife and a mother-in-law. Paul also wanted us to know this when he wrote to the Corinthians: "Don't we have the right to take a believing wife along with us, as do the other apostles and the Lord's brothers and Cephas (i.e., Peter)?" (1 Corinthians 9:5).

While sometimes we overdo the fact that scripture says as a response to Jesus' call to follow him, they left everything and followed, we can say here that answering God's call on our lives doesn't mean we must join a monastic order. The call most often asks us to return to our daily lives and vocations and let our new discipleship permeate them and make a difference. It comforts me and I take great satisfaction in knowing those who were the closest to Jesus were people of family and home and all the problems which go with that. Even more important is the fact that Jesus grew up in a family — brothers, sisters, parents, and all which that entails.

Peter's mother-in-law didn't rush to church after the healing. Instead she did, no doubt in a better way even, what she always did. She served her guests in her overcrowded, little home next to

44

the synagogue. Can't you just picture her preparing the bread and fish and wine with a certain joy? I hope Peter and Andrew offered to help, but I doubt it.

Sometimes when I look at this healing, I wonder if it might have been told over the years in order to say *there is in our discipleship strength for tired Christians.* As Jesus took her hand and removed the high fever, so he would take our hand when we are in our bed of weariness and help us up to give us the joy of serving again. I doubt any Bible scholar would affirm this idea from this story, but it helps me when I'm just plain tired doing the Lord's work and when, like Jesus that noon, people and demands keep coming at me from all sides. In Isaiah 40:28, 29, 31, we read these words in the Old Testament which our church mothers and fathers selected to go with the miracle story: "He will not grow tired or weary, and his understanding no one can fathom. He gives strength to the weary and increases the power of the weak ... those who hope in the Lord will renew their strength."

We know, too, that the one most blessed by service is not the one served but the one who does the serving. That's one of the reasons it's such a joy to be part of a congregation which is busy serving others way beyond just caring for their own. As a preacher most benefits from the preaching, a teacher from the teaching, and a witness from the witnessing, so too, the one who serves others benefits most not because one expects it, but because that's the way it is when you serve. I call it flip side theology. At Bishop's Cafeteria in Des Moines, Iowa, there is a light on each table. When you push the button the light comes on and the table waiter knows you want service of some kind. The sign says, "For further service, press button." The light of Christ calls us to further service. Simon Peter's mother-in-law knew it well.

What a tightly packed dynamite miracle that happened in a home next to the Capernaum synagogue on the north shore of the Sea of Galilee that Sabbath! The one who served the Christ was most blessed; there is new strength for tired Christians; the power of God experienced in church can also be in our homes; and we are saved to serve.

Three years after this miracle, I can picture a bent over, faithful, old Capernaum woman with scoured hands from years of hard kitchen work, who was, unlike most Galileans, malaria-free, and from her humble home with a flat, patched roof and an abandoned paralytic's stretcher out front, made her way each day to the nearby synagogue to do what she could as a woman back then to help with the ministry. On the Friday after Passover about 3 o'clock, she wailed a mournful cry as she had earlier that morning at cockcrow. The whole village winced as the pain of the cry pierced their hearts.

On the first day of the next week early in the morning there was a different sound which also came from her. It seemed to be even louder and more jubilant for that old, weak, and humble woman to make. As it echoed through the wadies and skipped across the mirror-like lake's surface, it sounded almost like a disguised hallelujah. And for a second time, the town gathered at her door. This early matriarch and saint of the little synagogue moved again more quickly than she had for several years. There would be fish to catch and fry. Her house and her family would never be the same again. Thank God the fever would not return.

Bringing The
Paralyzed To Christ

Mark 2:1-12

A hole-patched Capernaum roof reminded many who saw
one paralyzed with guilt and near bitterness of life,
whom friends willingly transported on invalid's stretcher.
We, too, must give up fault-finding and celebrate healing.

Late that evening, by a Capernaum neon light, no doubt, Peter
and his brother, Andrew, had some roof patching to do on their
mother-in-law's house. There may have had to be other repairs
also, from that crowd jamming the inside and outside to get a look
at and hear this new wonder worker of Galilee.

According to the way Peter described it to Mark, who later wrote
it down, the action had been mind-boggling, swift, and dramatic.
John baptized his cousin, Jesus, in the Jordan; Jesus was tempted
and decided his style of ministry; the disciples were enlisted; and
demons were driven out in the synagogue. Peter's mother-in-law
was healed. Sick and demon-possessed people were brought to Jesus
for healing. The crowds got larger and larger until they had to try to
hide for some rest ... but were pursued. Then there was this man
who had that dreaded leprosy. Jesus healed him also and told him to
keep quiet about it. But, understandably, he told it everywhere.

That brings us up to today's wonderful story of guilt, forgiveness, overcoming obstacles and severe criticism while doing the
right thing. Then there is the miracle of healing on the basis of
someone else's faith.

There was this man in the village who was paralyzed. He had four awfully good friends who loaded him on a stretcher and carried him to where the crowds had once again gathered to hear this new wonder worker. It was a crowded, chaotic scene. They couldn't get close enough even to catch the eye of Jesus, so they went up the outside stairway of the matchbox-like house and on the flat roof. There it wasn't a very big task to remove the mud and stocks between the rafters of the ceiling. They let their paralyzed friend down right in front of Jesus.

Wow! What gumption! What ingenuity! What determination to overcome the unexpected obstacles. Those who look for moral lessons in Jesus' miracles often point to these four who persisted perhaps even over the paralyzed's protest to give up and go home. Almost bordering on stubbornness they prevailed and Jesus rewarded them for it.

There are times in our Christian lives when we, like those same disciples, would fish all night in that nearby lake and catch nothing. But, Jesus says, try again and again. God has not forsaken us and we must not give up.

I'm happy for that man who was made well, but I'm especially happy for those four who learned that day the blessings of bringing people to Jesus even when all kinds of obstacles try to prevent it.

The preacher disappoints us, the governing board makes foolish decision, there are quarrels among congregational members, the national organization makes unpopular pronouncements, and we're tempted to think it's just not worth it to try any longer to bring people here. However, when we continue, God's spirit sees us through and successful, and we know the joy of not giving up or in. There were at least five houses in Capernaum full of celebration that night while Peter and Andrew patched their mother-in-law's roof.

Mark probably told this story and placed it here to prove the power of this Jesus. Right up front he claimed the power to forgive sins. The Old Testament had promised through Isaiah, "See, I am doing a new thing." Then, "... even I am he who blots out your transgressions ... and remembers your sins no more" (Isaiah 43:19, 25). The coming for the new kingdom meant for Mark, above everything else, plenty of free forgiveness. So he told this story here because he no doubt heard Peter preach it many times.

Often in our sophistication we Christians not only neglect to talk about how real sin is and how all pervasive it is in our lives; but we have all but eliminated from our worship the Holy Communion rites of the church to confess and have absolution declared to us. Yet here in this miracle is the clear message Jesus did come to work forgiveness for us as surely as he did to the consternation of the teachers of the law who were to investigate him.

Other well-meaning institutions and individuals can do many things for us humans, but here is the business of the church unique to its purpose and mission. That incident under the gaping hole in the mud roof was the beginning of what eventually sent Jesus to the cross, and going to that cross worked forgiveness, and that forgiveness God has entrusted to us contemporary disciples called the church to give out to all who will receive it.

It seems to me what happened that day may have been a guilt-ridden Galilean who so believed that sin produces illness that he thought himself into a paralysis. Jesus knew what was going on the minute those four resourceful men let him down from the ceiling. He didn't so much need medication or physical therapy. He needed forgiveness. And it's what so many of us still need today. It's what makes the church different from what those other organizations and professionals do. We offer forgiveness, God-riddance for guilt. The opportunity to get up from our crippled, debilitating mat and walk away clean and new. And you don't have to knock a hole in the church roof to have this free forgiveness. "He said to the paralytic, 'Son, your sins are forgiven'" (Mark 2:5b). From the cross Jesus forgives still. So, we have relief from the paralysis of guilt for such things as:

— cheating at our job, on our taxes or a test;
— being unfaithful to our spouse or a relationship;
— disappointing our parents or mentors;
— lying about our qualifications or position;
— doing a lousy job of parenting;
— giving in to an addiction;
— abusing the power we hold over someone else.

49

When the painful regret and haunting guilt riddle our psyche, we have a cure, confession and forgiveness — sweet forgiveness, the kind only God can give because of what God did in the person of Jesus on the cross. From the cross Jesus unloads us from that guilt which can paralyze. From the empty tomb he assures us we can start over. And from the Pentecost spirit, we know we have help to believe it all and accept this new equipment for life.

He says to us as he did to this man: " 'I tell you, get up, take your mat and go home.' He got up, took his mat and walked out in full view of them all. This amazed everyone ..." (Mark 2:11-12). It's an encouraging and comforting story that started with four determined men lowering this incorporated man into a jam-packed room of a humble house on the north shore of Galilee.

Often we can discover a flip side of the miracle stories. Records used to have two sides with one side the popular and better-known themes; if we turned them over there was often a less-known melody. That side was the flip side.

Perhaps the flip side to this miracle is the misery of those who came to find fault, and the wonderful assurance of Jesus in our homes.

Did you notice most everyone that day rejoiced that this paralyzed man had been healed? Mark writes, "This amazed everyone and they praised God, saying, 'We have never seen anything like this!' " (Mark 2:12b).

What a contrast! The crowd so happy for their neighbor and these few grumpy, old men criticizing how Jesus did it. The difference seemed to be that the larger group came expecting some great things to happen that day, and they did. On the other hand, there were these few who held power in the synagogue, seeing it challenged, who came very suspicious that this was too good to be true. You would think they would have been so pleased for this man. Instead, they split hairs over who could forgive sins and instead of calling the healing wonderful, they charged Jesus with blasphemy.

It can happen yet today. We can come to worship here expecting great things to happen. Or we can come suspicious and critical of everything and everyone. The former is so much more rewarding and happy a lifestyle than the latter. Fault is not hard to find, either. The fault finders will not only criticize, but will often dampen the efforts of those trying so hard to be faithful in their discipleship.

I wonder if it hurt Jesus that day when the criticism came from the pillars of that synagogue. When you are giving your best to help and then these fellows attack, it does hurt. And that's when the rest of us need to step in and affirm and support each other's imperfect efforts.

There is in this story a nice affirmation of Jesus in our home. Because Peter and Andrew invited him into their home it became a place of healing and forgiveness and comfort. That's the role that our homes ought to fulfill. Jesus teaching in the synagogue down the street is one thing. However, Jesus at home changes how we are and how others are blessed by our homes. Let the symbols be obvious, the prayers frequent, the witness open, that at the center of our homes is still the Christ.

Sometimes our homes can be a place of cruelty. Under our roofs we can forget how Jesus would have us treat each other. All the behaviors we applaud in church ought to be practiced all week long at home with family as well. Turn the other cheek, be kind to one another, pray for those who hurt you, are even more worthwhile and imperative at home.

Notice after the paralytic was healed Jesus told him: "I tell you, get up, take up your mat and go home" (Mark 2:11). I hope he went to his home not only rejoicing he had been healed but determined to be a different kind of person there as a response to that gift of health. And because he had been given undeserved forgiveness from Jesus, one would hope he would give it out undeserved to all in his home, family, and neighborhood who would receive it.

Exhausted, but happy, and quietly excited about their new discipleship, Peter and Andrew patched the hole in the roof of their mother-in-law's house late that night, perhaps with some help and supervision from her. They probably replaced the sticks and mud between the beams of the ceiling with overflowing hearts knowing that day in their home undeserved forgiveness had been given, a man paralyzed was cured, there was rejoicing in several other homes of those who had carried him there, and best of all, there was a family blessed whose father and husband had begun a whole new way to live, for Jesus had come home with him.

A Boat
For Rough Seas

Mark 4:35-41

When rough seas and wild storms rage about us,
there is one who can speak the word of blessed calm,
to still the turmoils which often so threaten us.
Yet, best of all, guide us through while winds rage on.

There are times when our lives are so very difficult, so fast and busy, and we are so tired we just want to get away for a while. It had been such a time for Jesus.

There are days when all kinds of struggle, pain, and misfortune enter our lives that we question if God cares or is even awake and notices. That's the way it was one early evening on the Sea of Galilee.

So Jesus said to his disciples, let's take one of these fishing boats and get away from this crowd so we can have a little peace and quiet. He no more got into the stern of the boat before he was sound asleep, exhausted from all the healing and teaching and pressure of the crowds who were now pursuing him.

That lake called Gennesaret is 680 feet below sea level, surrounded by deep gorges down which a cold wind rushes out and upon the calm sea with suddenness. The calm of one moment may be the raging storm of the next.

I have crossed over that lake several times and have seen the red flags which the boats with one mast and one triangular sail hoist in the bow to warn of this always present danger of storm.

So suddenly, what Mark calls "a furious squall came up" (Mark 4:37a). The small whitecaps became enormous waves which washed over the port and starboard gunnels. The boat was about to be swamped.

53

Those who heard Peter tell his eyewitness report of this frightening time wrote it down in their Gospel accounts for us to hear even today.

> *Jesus was in the stern, sleeping on a cushion. The disciples woke him and said to him, "Teacher, don't you care if we drown?" He got up, rebuked the wind and said to the waves, "Quiet! Be still!" Then the wind died down and it was completely calm.* — Mark 4:38-39

For 2,000 years we preachers have told and retold this familiar story as a wonderful miracle of rescue. The storm was evidently more than even those experienced Galilean sailors could handle, so Jesus, proving to them his power even over nature, told the wind and the water to be quiet. As frequently happens over a longer time period, it was calm.

There are wonderful things to learn from this frightening experience of the disciples.

Some would say the disciples told the story as proof that Jesus was really the powerful Messiah who the Old Testament had promised would come. The one about whom the psalmists wrote: "You rule over the surging sea; when its waves mount up, you still them" (Psalm 89:9).

Storms do come into all our lives no matter how strong our faith or how good our discipleship. And they can rage furiously, yet come unexpectedly and blow on and on and on.

In times like these we have a rescuer, one with great power to calm the furious water and wind.

Who here hasn't known the troubled water of deep sorrow, doubt, pain, anxiety, passion, temptation, and my big one — worry?

The plea of an old time gospel writer, Fanny Crosby, is often ours also: "Rescue the perishing, Care for the dying; Jesus is merciful, Jesus will save." A more contemporary song writer called our need "the bridge over troubled waters."

So the traditional, more conservative approach to this miracle of subduing wild storms into calm seas and wind is to draw the conclusion that to be in the same boat with Jesus is to have the seas calmed. It announces that whenever Jesus comes into life, its storms become quiet.

One writer said that this is a case of faith being tested and revealed like ours in all its frailty. Others offer words of profound comfort in saying that to be with Jesus means our storms will cease.

I'm just not sure this is the case. I think we have to question from our own experience whether Jesus calms our stormy situations of life. For instance, I wonder if the other boats along with Jesus' boat also experienced a calming of the sea that evening.

So here is the flip side of this miracle of Jesus: *Perhaps Jesus' calming was not so much the waves and the wind on Galilee that day, but rather the fear and panic in the hearts of those sailor-disciples.*

I've often wondered at the Transfiguration of our Lord upon the mountain — who really changed, the physical appearance of Jesus, or the disciples seeing him for the first time in a new light. So too here, I wonder if the storm didn't so much change as did the disciples' courage to get through it.

We all face the reality that no matter how religious we are, no matter how hard and often we ask God to take away our storms in life, they still rage on. What helps us weather the storm, no matter how frightening, fierce, and painful it may be, is God's presence and God's people with us.

Our rescue is not so much the absence of trouble, but rather, the presence of God, and I must add the presence of God's people as well.

It still hurts me severely to recall burying my oldest foster son. And even though she was old, giving up my beloved mother was very, very difficult.

Years ago when I first began my ministry and integrated an all-white congregation, how the storm of racism, hate, and disappointment raged around me. I prayed in those storms for rescue, but instead God gave the calm in my soul to survive and to sail on through those rough seas.

Three sons in Vietnam, one being wounded; struggles with other children; worry over finances; extremely frightening days in Liberia, West Africa, during a horrible, bloody tribal war; the discovery of cancer in my body and surgery for it — we all can draw a list.

Mine would not be nearly as long as many of yours. God doesn't remove the rough water, but God does place a hand on the helm to help steer us through to safe harbor.

We do have to ask here about the disciples' question to Jesus. In their panic and desperation, they said to the sleeping Christ: "Teacher, don't you care if we drown?" (Mark 4:38b).

We are often tempted to ask it in a similar fashion. "Hey God, don't you see my struggle here? I'm about to go under — are you asleep? Why don't you do something? How about a rescue?" Very much like the disciples, we cry out, "How about a little help here! Can't you see it's a bad storm?"

Sometimes we forget we may be the answer God provides in response to our own prayer. In an historical museum along the Mississippi River in Iowa, there is a sign at the helm of an old river boat which reads, "In a storm, pray toward heaven but row toward shore." There are times to pray and times to act on the prayer and actually become the way God answers it.[1]

Often we just don't recognize the help as it comes — perhaps a peace or calm which gets us through. Perhaps other of God's people steady us. Maybe at worship the calming assurance that we are loved unconditionally by God and by God's people gets us through a lot and motivates us to invite and welcome others into our boat, the Church of Jesus Christ.

It can be like the David and Goliath story related to us in 1 Samuel 17. The Philistine Goliath from Gath looked so big and strong, no Israelite soldier had the courage to fight there in the valley of Elah against him. David, however, saw him so big he just couldn't miss with his trusty slingshot.

The ship has always been a very ancient symbol for the Christian church. We even have Latin names for parts of our building which are parts of a ship, like nave and chancel. Both sides of this miracle tell me that in the church is the best place to be when life's storms come. It's also a wonderful place to be during calm sailing. But, when storms rage, we can make it to the other side or ride out the squall best in the church — where we have each other and the Christ is in our boat.

56

And let's be reminded that, like the traumatic evening on Lake Gennesaret when Jesus fell asleep and disciples panicked, the church can weather the meanest of storms. It may seem like it will swamp; it may seem like it will never get to the other shore. But with the Christ resting in the stern and disciples faithfully hard at work at the helm and working the sails, that old boat which has already survived so much and provided safe passage so well will do so again and again.

Divisions, quarrels, pastors disappointing us, conflicts over social positions, sinful greed, hurt egos, debates over insignificant issues, hurt feelings, financial crises, and hot tempers may all threaten to swamp the ship. But no matter how seasick we sailors become, we can sail on.

With God's word as our marker buoys to port and starboard, the ship and its passengers, no matter how rough the seas, will come through.

When Peter preached, it was always from the other side of this Galilee storm. He assured us the church will survive; the best place to be in a storm is in the same boat with the Christ. While this storm may not go away, there can be calm in our hearts. Our God has not been caught napping, but is here with us yet.

And now, confidently calm and secure, let's go out into our rough seas in God's peace.

---

1. Jerry L. Schmalenberger, *These Will Preach* (Lima, Ohio: CSS Publishing Co., 1999), p. 94.

Galilee's Hillside Sharing

Mark 6:30-34, 53-56

Jesus had compassion on the many hungry listeners,
and taught the wary disciples an unforgettable lesson
of response to need and how little becomes so much,
At his prompting they all participated in new sharing.

Matthew and Mark related this very special event which took place on the gradual slope of the north bank of the Sea of Galilee where the grass was still green. They should know as they had heard Peter's eye witness account. Young John may also have been there. He wrote about it, too, in the fourth Gospel.

It must have been a very memorable happening. It's the only miracle which all four Gospel writers put in their story.

The day was long, hot, and dusty when Jesus and his disciples needed some quiet time. They went across the north end of Galilee by boat to get away, only to have the restless eager crowd follow by the shore line.

It was supper time and they were hungry. The disciples had a familiar solution — "Send the people away so they can go to the surrounding countryside and villages and buy themselves something to eat" (Mark 6:36). Jesus no doubt surprised his disciples by telling them: "You give them something to eat" (Mark 6:37).

He had them get the crowd organized and begin distributing the five biscuits and a couple sardines. And lo, there was enough for everyone and even leftovers!

Wow! What a story — I would like to have been there. It was a fantastic experience for those disciples who handed out the food.

59

They never forgot it — at least three of the eye witnesses wrote it down for us to marvel over even today, 1,970 years later and halfway around the world from that green hillside.

Many will use this miracle of Jesus' feeding of the 5,000 as a proof Jesus was God's son and had the power to do some fantastic multiplication. They will marvel at his ability to multiply fish and bread, forgetting that sometimes God is accustomed to doing the same thing over a longer period of time using fish eggs and flour from wheat fields. Others will talk at length about verse 34 and the fact that Mark said "... he had compassion on them."

Those who see almost everything Jesus did as a fulfillment of the Old Testament Messiah will point to 2 Kings 4:43 and the words, "They will eat and have some left over."

It's tempting to rehearse again the traditional great lessons here. This miracle shows us human tendencies to react to human need — send them away, let someone else feed them. And our human reaction to resources — we don't have enough to make a difference. Not realizing that in God's hand a little can be plenty with even leftovers! Our resources are always adequate for the task — a lesson we disciples need to be reminded of over and over again.

Others would concentrate on this feeding as being like a sacrament when a tiny bit of bread is given to us and it satisfies our hunger for much, just as in Holy Communion.

If I were to preach on this obvious major side of the feeding of the 5,000, I'd want to point out and take great comfort in the proven fact that Jesus is interested in our physical needs as well as our spiritual ones.

If it were stewardship Sunday, I would surely point out our responsibility as stewards and disciples to bring to Jesus, even today, whatever we can and trust he will do great things with it. And to be good stewards of our leftovers also.

However, let's take a look at the flip side of this miracle of organization and feeding. While the gospel stories of miracles being performed by Jesus have a strong compelling message for us which has been told from the pulpits of our churches for centuries, there is also a back side — always a secondary message which can inspire and instruct us as well.

The flip side here is all about sharing. It's a way of discipleship, a lifestyle, a behavior which can shape who and how we are. It's an idea which is often contrary to what our contemporary culture applauds.

In a day when the secular world says to "stake out your turf," and "get what's coming to you," and "put me first," and "assert yourself," this miracle's flip side proclaims sharing all you have is what is fulfilling and God-like.

Perhaps on that Galilean hillside the event went like this: Almost everyone there had hidden away in his tunic, just above the leather belt in that little pouch all Palestinians have, his own bread, raisins, and fish, which is often the case. As the crowd got more and more hungry, no one was about to retrieve his own little meal. Then this young lad found by Andrew offered to share the two fish and five buns he had. Seeing his powerful example, others followed suit. Before long they had gathered in groups or rows of fifty or one hundred. And when they all shared what they had it was plenty — just as Jesus knew and the disciples doubted it would be.

While it's fun to marvel at Jesus' multiplying fish and bread, it's even more delightful to think what it means to share like those disciples and Jesus did on that late afternoon on Galilee's shore.

It's a message and lesson we North Americans need to hear over and over.

The flip side of this miracle speaks to us today who live in a country and culture of such abundance and wealth.

We so need in our practice of following Jesus, as his disciples, to give away large portions of what we have. There are hungry and homeless and powerless and those we disenfranchise in our community who have need. On God's behalf we must share, not hoard under our tunics, like those Jews that marvelous day in Galilee.

While children are suffering of malnutrition here, we wear our diamonds, drive our two or three cars, watch perhaps four or five television sets in our homes. Yet, this miracle points to exactly what we are to do — share.

There may be a flip side to the flip side in this miracle of Jesus: while we must share in order that Jesus' compassion is administered to those who have much less than we in this country and around the world, there may be an even more important reason for us to do it.

I believe those who share in large portion are the ones who most benefit from the sharing. We need to do it for our own spiritual health and sanity. We need to give away a lot in order that our Christian lives have the portionality they should have.

Let it be said here loud and clear: Those most blessed are the ones who do the giving. And while that's true, we don't do it for the wonderful effect it has on us — that blessing does inevitably come our way.

— It's an antidote for greed.
— It's a freeing from wealth-addiction.
— It's a consistency of deed to word.
— It's a spiritual blessing unexpected.
— It's a satisfying lifestyle.
— It's a way of discipleship which transforms us.

I doubt those disciples who distributed the bread and fish that day were ever the same again. While the crowd got a snack, the disciples got a new way of looking at their own resources, and a stewardship they didn't understand before. They learned real life is not hiding, hoarding, and protecting. It's giving oneself away and in lavish, trusting fashion.

From there they went on to learn the sharing life of a disciple also meant sharing the pain and joy of others. And we know it means sharing our world's resources in a way that assures resource inheritance for future generations. We, as disciples, must be good stewards of all that which God has provided us to live well in creation.

Our response is often that of the disciples: "Send the people away ..." (Mark 6:36a). A number of times, this was the response of the disciples. A woman wanted her daughter healed, an abrasive blind man, a leper, etc. And so, like those first disciples, we ignore and in a way send away rather than share with those who don't deserve it or those who will never appreciate it. Notice Jesus didn't say, "Give those who will thank us later something to eat." Or he didn't say, "Okay, take this bread and fish to the Lutherans or 'our people' or 'those not on welfare....' " You get the message. This is a grace meal for everyone who needs it. It was not one limited to those who deserved it or who are like us.

The flip side of this miracle of sharing may very well be larger than the main side! I take real delight in that. Because it gives us something to do and someone to be: a disciple who shares and who sees the possibilities in the small and insignificant.

Almost all we Americans have so much we can share: our money, our clothing, our food, our special talents, our joys and pain. And that's the way it ought to be as Jesus' disciples.

In order to keep this message close to the ground and practical, let me mention some of the sharing possibilities listed in your bulletin today:

— a spare room for a foster child or international exchange program;
— a turn at the homeless shelter or food bank;
— a portion of our allowance or of our pension for World Hunger;
— a second or third car for someone who has none;
— our time as an after-school tutor;
— a big brother or sister to someone who has none;
— our seldom used clothing to the thrift store;
— some of our books to an overseas library;
— paying the tuition for one of our seminary students.

Instead of sending them away to be on their own, we can take inventory and share what we have. If we all do, it will prove to be another miracle of abundance.

On the north slope of Lake Galilee that late afternoon, disciples who were there and those who heard an eye witness account wrote it down. It was a miracle of feeding the hungry and the flip side about disciples learning the blessings of sharing.

"They all ate and were satisfied ..." (Mark 6:42).

Sight For The
Blind And Persistent

Mark 10:46-52

Blind Bartimaeus was rewarded for faith and persistence,
and was given sight to follow the Christ in discipleship;
while we still puzzle why some are healed and others not.
We also learn God would not have us suffer on purpose.

His condition was a wretched one. Father Timaeus would have to lead him out to the dusty, hot roadside of Jericho so he could spend his days howling for charity to those who passed by on their way to Jerusalem. The response was often hateful.

Bartimaeus was blind. It was a common illness most often called ophthalmia, caused by the strong glare of the sun. Flies were everywhere. They often settled on the matter-encrusted eyes of the blind and spread the infection. On the Jericho road today, Christians still maintain a large vocational school for blind Bartimaeuses. On Mount Scopus, next to the Mount of the Ascension, we maintain Augusta Victoria Hospital where Arabs receive the miracles of modern medicine, including sight for some who had been blind.

No doubt Bartimaeus had heard of the Galilean who was working many miracles of healing and driving out demons. It was Passover time and since all male Jews had to attend in Jerusalem, he figured the rumors may be true that wonder-worker Jesus and his followers would be coming his way soon. He asked each time a little crowd passed by if that might be the man from Nazareth. Finally, the word came that it was Jesus surrounded by disciples and learners.

Like *20/20's* Barbara Walters described the late country singer Tammy Wynette's voice as "the cry of her voice," so there was a cry in this voice as well. It was hard to ignore. "He began to shout, 'Jesus, Son of David, have mercy on me!' " (Mark 10:47b). The students could not hear Jesus for these cries, and besides, this rebel Jesus who was challenging the orthodox religion of Palestine was on his last walk to the very center of his opposition. There were much more important considerations for Jesus that day than one of many obnoxious street-side beggars. Besides, they really didn't want to get mixed up with the title he used for Jesus, which meant he was the one who was promised to come and save the country. No doubt there were Roman soldiers lurking about and they would not take kindly to such revolutionary talk. So they "... told him to be quiet, but he shouted all the more, 'Son of David, have mercy on me!' " (Mark 10:48).

Here the story takes on a surprising turn. Unlike the Levite in the parable of the Good Samaritan, Jesus did not pass by on the other side of the road. Mark says Jesus simply said of the blind beggar, "Call him." Then Mark continues with what I like a lot. "So they called the blind man, 'Cheer up! On your feet! He's calling you.' Throwing his cloak aside, he jumped to his feet and came to Jesus" (Mark 10:49, 50).

If nothing else, this story told by three Gospel writers sets us an example about how we must treat those in our day who are challenged by some handicap. They obviously are very special in God's sight and we who can call them to the Christ and cheer them up must make a special intentional effort to do so. A ministry to and with them will both please God and bless us. And also there are those who are the social outcasts of our society. One only has to walk down a street in any of our major cities to see them, often in filthy clothing, matted hair, sleeping in the doorways and on the sidewalks at night and pushing their rusty grocery carts, pan-handling, asking for some charity from us as did Bartimaeus that day. Our temptation is to follow the example of those disciples by branding them "no goods," "mental patients," "alcoholics," and "drug addicts" and pass legislation to keep them from bothering us on the way to church or during our daily routines. There are many ways we directly or indirectly tell the misfits not like us to be quiet and stay out of sight. Often our congregations are not places of welcome for them. But abrasive, unpleasant, obnoxious as these sons and daughters of Timaeus may be, they are still God's children and we must find out the best ways to minister to them on God's behalf.

So Jesus asked Bartimaeus what he wanted. The answer was obvious. He wanted to see. And Jesus assured him he would see! And he did see! "Immediately he received his sight and followed Jesus along the road" (Mark 10:52b).

This blind beggar was very important to Jesus. On his way to the Jerusalem cross, he stopped the whole procession and gave him his sight back. How that was accomplished isn't all that important. Because Matthew said that Jesus touched the man's eyes, perhaps that touching involved wiping away the encrusted matter that for years had distorted his vision. We do know many today receive back their sight through miraculous new scientific methods which have been discovered by learning of God's natural laws. It's not quite as astonishing now, but just as great a gift for the blind to receive their sight.

However it happened, it happened. Three of the Gospel writers included it in their account of Jesus' life. It was, as the songwriter described, "Amazing grace, how sweet the sound that saved a wretch like me; I once was lost but now am found, was blind but now I see."

There is a precious love of the unlovely here by Jesus that makes it a powerful moment on that Jericho road. There is also a persistence on the part of Bartimaeus which paid off. He was not resigned to a meek acceptance of his state. They told him to be quiet and he wouldn't. He shouted and shouted only to be unheard. But he persisted and won the prize of sight.

Often we stop just short of the miraculous in our own lives. We make a rather timid request of God and then when something doesn't change right away, give up, saying, "we knew it wasn't any use in the first place." But this story says to persist. Shout out to the Christ. Make your request over and over, and in bold terms so that Jesus might also say of us, "What do you want me to do for you?" And then, "Go, your faith has healed you" (Mark 10:51-52).

As this story of giving sight to the blind has been told over and over, the last couple thousand years we preachers have pointed with great delight to that last sentence which says: "Immediately he received his sight and *followed Jesus* along the road" (Mark 10:52b). So here is a proper response to that gift of healing just like that of Simon Peter's mother-in-law in her home in Capernaum. She got up after Jesus cured her of her fever and served him. Bartimaeus, according to those who were there, followed Jesus. His healing meant his discipleship. Can't you picture this one-time blind beggar staying right close to Jesus as they climbed the road up toward Jerusalem? He probably drank deeply of every word of the one who had given him sight. He probably took in every visual impression along the way. And shortly after this he may have been one of the witnesses to Jesus calling forth another person. This time it was the Lord's best friend out of the grave at Bethany. What a sight that must have been for his newly regained eyes to take in!

It's something we must think about today. Because Jesus has done even more for us than he did one day a long time ago halfway around the world for Bartimaeus. The crucifixion came later for our complete, undeserved forgiveness, and the Easter resurrection followed after it by three days, so we gained the hope of life beyond the grave as well. Pentecost came still later to assure God's Holy Spirit with us now to face whatever life deals to us here.

So, you see, we too must join Bartimaeus on the road following Jesus. That reveals the stages of discipleship. It begins with our need, continues with gratitude, and is completed with unswerving loyalty. Regardless of the character and personality of the preacher, regardless of whether they sing the hymns we like, regardless of the friendliness or coldness of the congregation — we remain faithful to the Christ who called us and gave us sight that we might know forgiveness, eternal life, and God's spirit to see us through in the meantime. We serve because he has gifted us greatly.

I believe Bartimaeus stuck with it. I hope he was there with Jesus on Palm Sunday for his eyes to see the Savior go into Jerusalem. I hope his new eyes were there at Calvary and in the Easter garden and on the Emmaus road and in the upper room and at exciting, spirit-filled Pentecost. I hope he and his father were part of the leadership of that early church, holding meetings in their humble home in Jericho.

Peter Jennings of *ABC News* announced his series about the millennium and the passing of a century with these words, "The familiar story is not the whole story." So in looking at the miracles of Jesus, the usual interpretation is not all there is to consider. We can often be instructed by a flip side or other side of the story not so obvious and perhaps not even intended by the narrative writers. It seems there are two we need to consider here: *Why do some have to suffer like this beggar and others have it so good? And the second is, when we get out of the church building and out in the world, all kinds of new opportunities come to us for doing Christ's ministry as his committed disciples.*

A couple of years ago while eating at a Wendy's restaurant in Mesa, Arizona, my wife spotted an older, tan-colored Ford van equipped with a wheelchair lift. The Arizona plates said it all: Y-ME. I'll bet Timaeus often asked it of his God, "Why me, Lord? Why do I have to be the one who has the blind son I have to care for all his days? I've been faithful in keeping the law and worshiping in your temple. Why do I have to be the one to suffer?" And no doubt, son Bartimaeus asked the same question as he held his position along that hot, cruel Jericho road, too.

Job had asked the question years before and we ask it in our time of affliction. There is no perfect answer but this much I can promise you: there is a difference between what God wants to happen to us and what God permits to happen to us. Except in the miracles, God is not fickle but very dependable as to how things operate in natural law. Physicians depend on this in order to practice good medicine. We count on this in many elements of our lives. When two cars crash head on at high speed, every time there will be drastic results. So that doesn't mean God wanted us to be in the accident. I'll say it again for father Timaeus' and son Bartimaeus' benefit — there is a difference between what God permits and what God causes to happen to us. God did not want Bartimaeus to be blind. God did not want Timaeus to have to deal with a blind son.

69

Still, like Job, there was a confidence that in this instance God would step in and change the circumstances. "I know that you can do all things; no plan of yours can be thwarted" (Job 42:2).

The thing I most celebrate in this story and is probably more the fact I want to proclaim than the miracle's integral teaching is this: great things can happen when we get out of the safety of the church building and into the world with our religion. It's so easy to keep our witness and practice of the faith here in the sanctuary where it is much less embarrassing to do it.

Here, when Jesus finally gave up on teaching in the synagogues and got out in the real world, dramatic, dynamic things were possible. On this try alone, lepers were cleansed, the dead raised, disciples recruited, new life given Zacchaeus, a parade organized and, of course, Bartimaeus given sight.

We modern day disciples can accomplish great things, also. We need take our dynamic faith out to our homes, neighborhoods, places of employment, schools, restaurants, bars, and places of rest and recreation. Our faith is not practiced like a "base-hugger" in the game hide-and-seek. When we finish here, it's out into this week's secular world where we live, work, and play. It is there we can, like Jesus' disciples, "call him" to the Savior, carry out our ministry in obedience to his command. Wonders and miracles are still possible outside the church. Let's take our witness and prayers, compassion and the Holy Spirit with us today as we move out to live among the Bartimaeuses of our day. We have a message to give to all who will listen, similar to the one Jesus told the disciples to deliver. "Cheer up! On your feet! He's calling you" (Mark 10:49b). The outside world is hungry for these words and we have them to offer. That's quite a flip side to a miracle about persistence: giving sight and trying to keep the abrasive out of our sight! It adds the realistic question of "Why me?" and the challenge to go public with our very private faith.

Bartimaeus' condition was a wretched one, but Jesus heard his plea and gave sight. And Timaeus turned cartwheels on his old limbs all the way home that night as his son headed up to Jerusalem, determined to follow the Savior.

New Life For
A Dead Friend

John 11:32-44; Isaiah 25:6-9

---

*The stench of death surrounded Christ's sorrow, crying
with sisters' disappointment in him very moving,
from the dead Lazarus and new life requisitioned.
Our call comes to exit the dark caves which entomb us.*

Some scholars try to explain this extraordinary Bethany story
with terms like: a trance, a hoax, allegory, teaching amplification of
Dives and Lazarus, and a whole bunch of other rationalizations. I'll
admit I'm not sure what all happened those four days at the home
of Mary, Martha, and Lazarus either. But I am sure it was of great
magnitude and consequence for them and for us here now.

This home was where Jesus went sometimes when he had business three miles away in Jerusalem. It was a retreat for him and
his disciples when they needed some peace and quiet and good,
warm friendship.

Lazarus was a good friend. Some think he was the beloved
disciple the scripture talks about. When he became ill, his sisters
sent word to Jesus. But Jesus did not go to him right away, perhaps
because his critics had tried to explain away the other miracles of
life for the dead, like the daughter of Jairus or the widow's son at
Nain. Because they said these people really hadn't died yet, Jesus
decided to let Lazarus die and be dead before he came to do anything about it. Or perhaps it was simply a matter of having such
pressing crowds and needs of others that he simply, like we do on
occasion, waited too long.

What one of us hasn't waited too long to come to the aid of a
friend only to find when we did that it was sadly too, too late? And

71

how much that hurts when we realize we have let down a friend who was counting on us.

In Palestine, there was no waiting for burial. Because of the hot climate, the decay was quick and the dead were buried on the day they died. So when Jesus did arrive, his friend had been dead and buried already four days. Martha and Mary told him the grim news. He must have felt terrible. In fact, John says, "Jesus wept" (John 11:35). It's the shortest verse in the Bible. Just two words, but it tells us so much about God and about our relationship to God. I have quoted it so often by grave side or at the foot of the casket, for this tells us we are loved. It tells us God, because of Jesus, knows what it is to lose a loved one. One of the greatest things Jesus did was to bring us the news of a God who cares. That's comforting to me. When I cried at our oldest son's burial, at my mother's funeral, and at the memorial service of my best friend, it helped a lot to know not only that they are okay in their life beyond their graves, but that God knows how much it hurts to lose a loved one.

To the Greeks for whom this Gospel of John was written, this was a delightful surprise. Up until that time they thought of God as unfeeling and without compassion. What a different picture of God Jesus proclaims with his tears! Here is one who really cares. Here is one who feels the agony and pain. Here is a God who even knows what it's like to disappoint someone who was counting on him. Hear again the poignant words of Mary, "Lord, if you had been here, my brother would not have died" (John 11:32b). Those mourners standing nearby said, "See how he loved him!" (John 11:36).

That's the way it ought to be. People who loved them gathering to give loving comfort and support when into their midst the Christ came, feeling the pain, loss, and disappointment and being, according to John, "... deeply moved in spirit" (John 11:33b). And crying. Since that day in Bethany at the home of Mary and Martha and Jesus' beloved disciple, we now will never have to face the loss of death alone.

And there is hope. It is a hope which is definite and encouraging. It looks like John told this story to make sure we know that Jesus demonstrated what it's like in God's kingdom and that he assures those who would read about it that death is not the end. The miracle of Lazarus' resurrection surely points us to Easter a few days later a few miles from there. John no doubt saw what happened that day as a proof that what Isaiah had promised years before was now taking place.

"On this mountain he will destroy the shroud that enfolds all peoples ... he will swallow up death forever. The Sovereign Lord will wipe away the tears from all faces" (Isaiah 25:7-8).

It was a deliberate act claiming Jesus as Lord and brought many, many Jews to praise this Lord on Palm Sunday. It also, according to John, put in motion what eventually brought about the crucifixion of Jesus on the Friday next.

The die was cast. When they heard that many Jews put their faith in him, those who were threatened by this testimony of who Jesus was and what he could do had seen and heard enough. They said, "Here is this man performing many miraculous signs. If we let him go on like this, everyone will believe in him, and then the Romans will come and take away both our place and our nation" (John 11:47b-48).

Picture the contrasting scene. There were mourners crying, wailing, and shrieking almost hysterically. Jesus arrived and both Mary and Martha told him in bitter disappointment that he was too late. He was so troubled and moved he cried. Then they went to that cave-like tomb you can still see at Bethany. The round stone sealing the entrance is rolled in its groove to open the grave. Martha gasped out a warning that by now there would be an awful stink from the decaying body. But Jesus persisted because he wanted them to see God's glory. And they did see God's glory like never, ever before! There was a spine-tingling anticipation and then the story rushed to a dramatic conclusion.

Listen to John's own words in describing what happened: "... Jesus called out in a loud voice, 'Lazarus, come out!' The dead man came out, his hands and feet wrapped with strips of linen, and a cloth around his face. Jesus said to them, 'Take off the grave clothes and let him go' " (John 11:43-44).

So those who expected a motionless, rotting corpse saw instead, stumbling out of that dark rock-hewn inner chamber, a vital

73

living man still wrapped in strips of cloth, pulling them off so he could see, walk, and live again. It must have been an astonishing sight, seeing this alive-again body pulling off the burial wrappings so he could move freely once more.

Think what that sight meant to his sisters, Mary and Martha, and think how grand it must have been for Jesus to see the man so dear to him coming out. But, most of all, think what this traumatic event was like for Lazarus!

And that's the other side of this miracle which took place in Jerusalem's little suburb now called Azariyeh, which is derived from the name Lazarus. There is a secondary message here, in addition to those of God caring about us, death not being the end — we do have a resurrection and a glimpse of God's glory. I like best the part about this man responding to Jesus and coming out of the cave which had entombed him.

Would you consider this flip side of the Bethany miracle with me for a few moments? It's probably not what will be emphasized in many pulpits today, but perhaps very important for us and our congregation.

There is help for us when (and as) we are entombed in our own lives in our little towns and big cities today. *And there are many caves from which we need to hear Jesus call us to come out.* We too, like Lazarus, whose common name was Eleazar (meaning God helps), have need to come out of our caves of darkness and take off the grave clothes to be freed and let go.

There is something about our culture, modern lifestyle, and basic human nature which allows us to be entombed by a sort of death while still alive. We also need a Savior who calls us out of our graves and caves. Today I especially think of addictions which are so seductive and would wrap us in grave clothes and imprison us in narrow black caves, restricting our potential of being the full, loving person God would have us be.

There is the cave of hunger for power which opposes God so effectively to entomb us. There is that awful addiction to drugs which distorts how we and life can be, engulfing us in the wrappings of death. Then there is perhaps the most deadly one of all in our U.S. culture: the addiction to wealth which entombs us into false priorities of greed. There is that attractive lust for sexual pleasure outside our marriage covenant which kills our relationship of fidelity with our spouse. And, of course, everywhere in the world and certainly in Bethany today, there is always present the narrow cave of racial prejudice which perverts love of neighbor and richness of the diversity of God's creation into a morbid hate which destroys us even more than its object.

To all these and whatever else imprisons us, this story says on the flip side that with Jesus' help we can, like his dear friend Lazarus, hear the call: "... come out! ... Take off the grave clothes and let him go" (John 11:43b, 44b).

I sense a certain new freedom of movement and being for Lazarus which is also available to us because the story really didn't stop at Bethany. On the Sunday of the Passion, Jesus and the disciples went on to Jerusalem, then to the cross, then from another very similar grave (I wonder if Lazarus was there to call him out?), then perhaps best of all to return in spirit to make available to us this God's glory and power, demonstrated so long ago.

It is only with this available equipment for life which the spirit gives us that we can hear the voice calling us out and we can break loose from those things of sin which want to entomb us.

Let that be our prayer today and this week: we rejoice that we have eternal life; we celebrate having a loving, caring, forgiving God with us; we enjoy the glory of that God witnessed here.

And on the flip side, we are called out of our tombs of sin to a new life with other disciples and the Christ who says, "I am the resurrection *and the life*. He (or she) who believes in me *will* live ..." (John 11:25).

I, with John, would have told us just a little more of the story and about Lazarus' life after this resurrection. Was he there shouting hallelujah on Palm Sunday? Was he there when Judas betrayed Jesus, and did he stand by Peter when he tried to defend him in the garden? Did he and his sisters go that Easter night to the upper room to be with the other believers? And on Pentecost, was he one of those preaching like tongues of fire? Do you suppose Mary, Martha, and Lazarus started meetings in their home for believers?

And the second time he died, do you suppose there was a low moan from him which said, "Been there, done that!"?

Let the scholars debate whether it's a trance or a hoax, allegory or other theories to explain it away. You and I and John know something tremendous happened that day in Bethany, and it gives us renewed hope and changed lives even today as we hear the call, "Come out and take off your grave clothes and live!"

Capernaum's Favorite Centurion

Luke 7:1-10; 2 Kings 18:20-39

The loving concern of a Gentile centurion's ill servant,
is a model of how God would have us treat each other.
This great faith rewarded with healing at a distance.
In joy we must share our wealth and love across the races.

Only a few times in the life of Jesus is it recorded that he complimented someone. Today in the Capernaum story of healing at a distance, we have perhaps the strongest one of all. And it was about not a rabbi or disciple or priest or even his mother or Peter's mother-in-law. It was for a Centurion! Listen: "I tell you, I have not found such great faith even in Israel" (Luke 7:9b).

Certainly the focus and heart of this story is not a healing at a distance or even that it was a slave who was healed. The story centers around an attitude, the attitude of a Roman centurion garrisoned in Capernaum and sympathetic to Jews. This amazed Jesus and no doubt Luke who wrote it down for our astonishment.

Here's how it went, according to Luke and Matthew as well. A small group of town elders came to Jesus and asked if he would work one of his healing miracles on the slave of a local Roman who treated them well and even built the church for the town. So Jesus set out for the Centurion's house, but before he got there, the Centurion sent another messenger to say it wasn't necessary to come into the house of a Roman (something forbidden for Jews) but just to say the word and he knew his dear slave would be okay. That's when Jesus said this was such an amazing fellow — he had better faith than anyone he'd met so far in all of Israel. At that moment the slave who was so important to his Centurion master was healed.

In most stories of healing, we like to go right to the marvelous thing that happened for the one who was ill. In this case it's about attitude, I believe, which Luke wanted us to see and understand.

I remember a plumber I liked very much who used to call his cocktail time "attitude adjustment time." This story so commends certain attitudes of this Roman soldier, perhaps this sermon time can be an attitude adjustment time for you and me. Luke would really like that.

Slaves in that day were thought of as tools, disposable when no longer useful. The master had complete authority over them. It was the very different attitude of this "God-fearer" Gentile who sent the request. He loved his long-time servant. His servant's suffering was his suffering. He couldn't bear the thought of losing this person who had given so much of his life in loving service to him — so came the unusual request and successful reward for caring and asking.

This really calls for attitude adjustment. While we don't have slaves anymore, many of us do have those who serve us in one fashion or another. Some here are employers, others manage employees, still others simply exercise the power necessary to keep folks under their supervision. This Capernaum long-distance healing of a slave tells us we ought to have a sense of loving stewardship as we carry out our responsibilities which put us in charge of others' welfare and very existence. The foreman, the supervisor, the CEO, board members, and union stewards all ought to see their vocation as a ministry to their people for whom they have charge. It's what Jesus commended when he said to those following nearby, "I tell you, I have not found such great faith even in Israel" (Luke 7:9b). The challenge here is to adjust our attitude to carry out those principles of behaviors Jesus asks for in church to our supervisor's positions all week. It is there we put these into radical practice in real life: be kind one to another, turn the other cheek, pray for your enemies, and go the extra mile. Now *that's* radical attitude change! By the way, there are modern new management theories now being taught which claim this is a more productive way to treat employees anyway.

Here's another attitude that was so different. Not only did this Centurion care compassionately about his slave, he also loved the Jewish people. That's different. Usually the Jews hated the Romans who occupied their land; and in turn, the Romans hated the Jews who had such strange practices like not eating good pork, loafing on the Sabbath, and believing only they had the correct religion. This Roman was so wrapped up in the Jewish Capernaum community he built their church. No wonder the town elders came with this request on his behalf, and no wonder Jesus gaped in amazement as he headed off to see if he could help.

One of the saddest elements in our sinful human nature is prejudice and race hatred. It is at the root of many of our horrible wars; it continues to tear communities asunder; and it perverts the way God created us to be and how God would have us enjoy the richness of the diversity of creation. I personally believe it is one of the most effective ways the demonic force against God and good still permeates our humanity. Ethnic cleansing, job discrimination, civil rights abuse, subtle housing regulations, and on and on the list could go. And often it is strongest in God's church!

Why is it that our very nature seems to seduce us to act in this way? It seems we want to feel we are better than another color, class, gender, nationality, or religion. We seem to get our sense of worthiness by putting someone else below us. It is demonic. Jesus will have none of it — and neither did a humble Capernaum Centurion whom Jesus so admired. He loved his slave. He loved the local Jews. And he deeply respected a Jewish Galilean named Jesus.

The miracle here is that a Jew cared about a Gentile and a Gentile loved a Jew! That takes real attitude adjustment.

There is yet another attitude to be admired here. It's the confident faith this Roman had in Jesus. He sent word that he knew what it was like to have authority and Jesus had a lot more than he did. So he needn't even bother coming to the house. Just say the word and he was confident the beloved slave would be well again. He was sure Jesus didn't need touch, use clay and spit, see in person, pray over, or anything prescribed by the Jewish law — "just say it, Jesus, and my slave will be fine!" — and he was!

Faith does make a difference, doesn't it? I wonder how many Capernaum sick weren't healed that day because no one had the faith to request it? If ever there was a story of the miraculous which encouraged us to pray for the sick, it's this one. If we believe, God is able to do wonderful things not only for us, but wonderfully so for those we care about who may not even know Jesus. Here is our mandate, to ask. Here is an affirmation to pray for others regardless of their faith, or lack of it.

When in Neuendettelsau, Germany, recently I received the devastating news that cousin Gretel from Schmalenberg had been in a horrible car accident. Pastor Moser called me with the news that she had thirteen broken bones and a broken neck and was near death in a hospital in Mannheim. As an American pastor, I told them I would come at once to pray by her bedside. To my surprise, Uncle August and husband Peter agreed I should not come. I was so hurt by their attitude. Then I learned that, at least in the Rhein/Pfaltz, when a priest came to the hospital to pray it meant the patient would die. So they didn't want me to frighten my favorite German cousin. She lives now, thank God. I must one day soon tell her about this miracle of asking for recovery and getting it. And I must somehow introduce a far different attitude about prayer, its purpose, and the wonderful possibilities that are available with faith.

For every story there must be another side than the one which is the more obvious. I call it the flip side. In this story there are two less familiar melodies I'd like to play for you on the flip side of the ancient record. These are *how we treat and what we believe about other religions, and the financial stewardship of giving away wealth as the Centurion did.*

There never have been any people so shamefully treated, so misunderstood, so persecuted, so hated as the Jews. We Christians have contributed, or at least remained silent, while horrible crimes against them were committed. Our own reformer, Martin Luther, said hateful things about them we wish he had never said or written down. We must be ashamed. The shadow of the Holocaust in Germany where I wrote this sermon is still a dreadful stain on our practice of discipleship.

In this story Jesus, a Jew, heals a Roman pagan's servant. The Roman servant loved and had faith in the Jew. That's the attitude we must make. Because we believe that for us the new covenant to be in Christ is the only way to salvation, we have forgotten that Jews have always been a very favorite people to God. They, too, have a promise, a covenant with God. It's not as comforting or grace-filled as ours, but it's valid and we ought to respect and affirm their covenant for them just as we affirm ours for ourselves. We also must examine what and how we teach about the life of Jesus in our Sunday School, Christian Education classes, and Bible studies. We could be, without realizing it, putting dislike for Jews into the minds of our children and older adults. I'm not sure how certain that belief is in our Christian theology and I am sure there are many who will rail against it by quoting verses only from the New Testament. Perhaps it's not yet the official teaching of our denomination, either. In the light of this miracle story, it seems so right to me. Enough putting down of other religions or denominations. Let's see like Jesus instead, what we can be amazed with about their faith. As the world becomes more and more a global village, we must make this change in attitude. Not to do so is a luxury we cannot afford, we who believe there is a God who wants to watch over us.

Perhaps it's time to admit that all religions are very, very important attempts to describe God and represent God in this world. So we must be patient, respectful, and Jesus-loving for all.

Isn't there in this flip side of the miracle something almost missed? This fellow, not a Jew, in a Jewish town donated the synagogue. How marvelous and miraculous. Already he was reaping the unexpected harvest of his benevolence. Of course the elders would ask Jesus for help on his behalf. They said to Jesus, "This man deserves to have you do this, because he loves our nation and has built our synagogue" (Luke 7:4b).

I recall visiting a very old Bible woman named Mama Gardner in Liberia, West Africa. She took us to an ugly, little mud and bamboo hut with a crooked cross on top. It was the village Christian church. The structure looked like it could accommodate about twelve to fourteen people. The old woman held out her arthritic hands and said, "I built it with my own hands. I told the people that where I live there *will* be a church." Suddenly the little edifice took on the appearance of a great cathedral! The Capernaum Centurion must have been of a similar determination and had gained the same respect.

Here is the encouragement we need to share our wealth, to see that the money we have earned and accumulated is not hoarded, but given away for the continuation of miracles in our day and in future generations. When we donate money to the church and its ministry around the world, there is such benefit to those who receive it. But there is also that unexpected blessing to the giver that always comes in great measure. As a congregation of believers we don't very often give enough of what we have to make the deed very meaningful to those who benefit or to ourselves. So we limp along, never knowing the profound joy which the Centurion who gave the people of Capernaum their synagogue knew.

If you are too frightened to do the sharing right now, think about your will and the words in it which will say one day: "He (she) loved our nation and has built our synagogue" (Luke 7:5). For the cause of elimination of world hunger, for desperately needed help for refugees, for the education of pastors, for Christian colleges, for the establishment of new congregations, and for sending missionaries to our partner churches around the world are only a few of the ways we can be like this man who gave so much to the Jews of Capernaum.

It need not be dramatic gifts either that can adjust our attitudes. The regular offerings at worship along with additional needs for the local ministry and church building are always a way to give — and to do it not because we are pressured, but in a way that brings joy and satisfaction all around.

We've found a lot in this rather simple story. There is this marvelous scene where Jesus compliments a Roman Centurion for his attitude toward his servant and the Jews, race and religious bigotry, faith in Jesus, and the handling of our money. Along with my favorite plumber, this has been quite an attitude adjustment time.

82

Let's not forget the healed servant. We rejoice in that as well. Luke simply puts it, "Then the men who had been sent returned to the house and found the servant well" (Luke 7:10). Let's now return to our houses with attitudes adjusted that we might also find wellness.

Compassion At Nain's East Gate

Luke 7:11-17; 1 Kings 17:18-24

At Nain's east gate a widow grieves her only son;
Jesus responded as Elijah had years before him,
demonstrating his great power over death and grave.
Modeled for us disciples a ministry of compassion.

The cold, snowy ride in the funeral coach from St. Michael's Church in Mifflin, Ohio, to the hilltop cemetery nearby seemed like it went on forever. It was our foster son killed by cancer whom we transported to his final resting place. To lose a family member is difficult, but to lose a son is almost unbearable. I remember the terrible ache in my heart and the ceaseless, salty tears which would not be stopped. If Jesus, I thought, could bring back the widow's son of Nain and of Zarephath, why not my oldest son with whom I had yet so much to hear, understand, and speak? But we arrived at the icy hilltop and the grim words were repeated, as if shouted over those fields and Mifflin Lake for all to hear the conclusion to his short life. "We commit his ashes to the ground, dust to dust, ashes to ashes...."

It was not the same for Nain's widow's son another day. As the disciples, Jesus, and a crowd walked up that only road to the gate of the city, they came upon a group of flute players and professional criers leading a late afternoon funeral procession to the nearby cemetery, which one can still see there to this day. Some men carried a dead boy, probably in a wicker-work basket. The words are poignant: "the only son of his mother, and she was a widow" (Luke 7:12b).

85

So Doctor Luke, always interested in health and healing, said not that the widow was a person of faith or, like the paralytic healed by Jesus, that those who carried him were faithful. He simply said, "When the Lord saw her, his heart went out to her and he said, 'Don't cry.' Then he went up and touched the coffin (a dramatic gesture as that made him unclean, according to the Jewish laws) and those carrying it stood still. He said, 'Young man, I say to you, get up!' The dead man sat up and began to talk, and Jesus gave him back to his mother" (Luke 7:13-14).

It's the loveliest story in all the Gospels. Luke probably wanted it known because it proved the power of Jesus like a prophet. You see, this wasn't the first time a Nain widow had her dead son rescued from the brink of death. In 1 Kings 17:18-24 we read how years before in a town then named Zarephath, the great, respected prophet Elijah took the only son of a widow (who had fed Elijah for some days) and brought him back from death. It was the same back-water village and the same east gate and the same threat of a mother losing her only means of comfort and support. So here was a direct claim for Jesus having great power, even over death, like Elijah before him.

While Jesus did not bring my son back to life at the village gate, I do find great comfort in the fact he was baptized into Christ and thus has God's care and the benefit of Jesus' victory over death. He does not remain in the cold earth tomb in which we placed him. I don't know the specifics of how it all works; but I do have the comfort that Jesus, who gave the widow back her son that day, also cares for my son this day. And perhaps the miracle is that the cancer no longer devours his lungs and brain, distorting the presence of our granddaughters' father. Now he is given a peace in a new life beyond that hilltop grave. While not here, our son lives again. Gradually perhaps we can celebrate it.

Some have tried to describe this miracle of Jesus like the healing of Jairus' daughter, one of diagnosis. Perhaps what the boy was saved from that day was being buried alive as many were, according to archaeological evidence found in Palestine's graves. It could be that Jesus saw the little lad was in a catatonic trance and woke him up. Maybe. But then again, perhaps it was simply that Jesus, seeing a mother in such anguish losing her only son and with him her means of support, and having the power he had, just couldn't help but bring the boy back. Notice Luke said of Jesus, "... his heart went out to her" (Luke 7:13). The original word here is one of the strongest in the New Testament Greek — it means "he felt deep compassion to the depth of his bowels."

That's the other thing we often emphasize. Jesus felt in his heart. God is not unfeeling as the stoics of his day claimed. We have a Savior who hurts for and with us. And not just for the high and mighty and those whose pictures are on *Time* and *Newsweek*. No, not only those featured on CNN and the Biography Channel, but a single mother whose only son had died. Ever since Nain's second great day at the city gate, in churches and funeral homes and cemeteries around the world, single mothers who must lay their sons to rest can take comfort. Jesus says not to cry, he will help. He hurts for us when we hurt. According to John's Gospel, Jesus told the disciples, "Because I live, you also will live" (John 14:19b). We who are disciples have that promise to cling to as well.

Consider with me the flip side of this story. Perhaps not only did Jesus feel deep compassion for this widow; but perhaps he knew he needed to prepare his disciples for a ministry of compassion. With the crowd and the superficial popularity which was his at the moment, no doubt those disciples were beginning to feel rather important. They show by their comments that they often thought Jesus ought not to waste his time on the individual insignificant person. "Lead them away, quiet him or her," etc., was their attitude. So Jesus had the opportunity at the gate of a little unimportant village, where the disciples didn't see the need to go, to demonstrate the beauty and godliness of graceful compassion.

If this seems far out, just remember that as far as we know, most of the disciples were men. We men often aren't given to expressions of compassion and tenderness like our often kinder and more sensitive women counterparts. Still, we live in a world of broken hearts who need our love and compassion. In our U.S. culture we often tell boys to be brave, and in indirect ways they learn from us that real men don't show their feelings or are not moved by others' hurts and grief. Often in an effort to be "manly" we brush off the opportunity to have God's compassion for someone who needs it and leave that to the women. So, this episode at Nain's gate, whether intended or not, showed these disciples a different way of relating to people. It was not on her merit or based on her status and prestige; it was simply the fact that someone hurt, Jesus identified with that, and helped with what he could do.

We disciples have such opportunities every day. The list could be long:

— The person we work next to is having problems with his marriage or his children.
— The next-door neighbor's parent dies.
— The friend of a friend has discovered he is HIV positive.
— We are confronted with a hungry, homeless person.
— We see on television refugees living in camps.
— A fellow student flunks an exam or loses a girlfriend.
— The local social service agency pleads for foster homes for children.
— A significant other unexpectedly moves out.
— A friend loses her job of many years.
— Divorce of parents rends the hearts of their children.

Like those widows for whom Elijah and Jesus had compassion, we must also. For it's the way Jesus counts on his love and compassion getting to those who have need of it. We are the conduits through which that deserved or undeserved love ought to flow. Our congregation, in addition, ought to be an even larger pipeline through which people who are suffering might receive this gift of grace.

On the CBS evening news concerning the helping of refugees, the newscaster said, "Americans are suffering from 'compassion fatigue.' " Probably those who passed by the beaten man in the ditch along the Jericho road were also. We just cannot allow ourselves to become tired of doing good and feeling the pain of others. Jesus counts on us to help. We must not permit the secular world's constant ridicule of "do-gooders and bleeding hearts" to deter us. Jesus says to watch him at Nain and then on his behalf, to do it.

A big fire at Thousand Oaks, California, was started by a homeless man trying to keep warm. Many million dollar homes burned to the ground. What irony. Perhaps those homeowners are the very same people who failed to care for this man. We pay a price whenever we ignore the poor and homeless. Eventually it comes back to our lives and homes. For as we have seen in so many of the things Jesus asks us to do, we who do these acts of mercy and compassion are the ones who most benefit.

To develop tough hide which is not moved by another's plight is often to shrink and whither in our discipleship as an individual and as a worshiping congregation of believers. If compassion fatigue has infected us here, let this story of Jesus caring about a widow from Nain losing her only son be a tonic that brings new life to our church and to us as individuals. It can do that. Whole congregations can be reorientated when they take on a special ministry of compassion like the resettlement of refugees or the feeding of the local hungry. Dramatically the focus is changed from looking inward, being critical, and getting one's own needs met, to reaching out and touching the unclean, bringing God's healing to them. And in so doing we are healed. The Nain miracle happens again! We fulfill what the apostle Paul asks his Colossian congregation to do: "... as God's chosen people, holy and dearly loved, clothe yourselves with compassion, kindness, humility, gentleness and patience ... And over all these virtues put on love ..." (Colossians 3:12, 14a).

Those ministries of compassion might include:
— to the hearing-impaired;
— to the homeless and emotionally disturbed;
— to battered women and abused children;
— to slow learners and those of other languages;
— to the elderly and alone;
— to the sick at home and physically-impaired;
— to estranged marriage partners;
— to the unemployed and underemployed;
— to those in prison and on parole.

These victims of life's tragedies await at Nain's gate for our compassion on God's behalf, too.

The one who went to the cross of Calvary for our forgiveness and came out of the grave felt such compassion for us imperfect sinners that he pleads for us to be kind people to each other and show the same compassion as he and Elijah at Nain.

There is yet another element in this miracle at Nain. I really don't know if the widow or the son even said thanks. Luke doesn't say whether these two who most benefitted from Jesus' compassion that day joined the others in praising God or not. The help Jesus gave was not given because they deserved it, as far as we know, or that they were grateful afterward. Like the healing of the ten lepers, the miracle was one of compassion and not out of any expectation to be thanked.

There goes one of our biggest excuses for not helping in our town and in our neighborhoods! We do it because God wants us to have compassion for all who hurt regardless of their lack of appreciation. A little earlier, Luke quoted Jesus in this light: "But love your enemies, do good to them, and lend to them without expecting to get anything back ... Be merciful, just as your Father is merciful" (Luke 6:35a, 36).

Perhaps burying a son or daughter is hardest of all. It was so for us when Art died. It was so for the widows of Zarephath and of Nain. They teach us something, however, we must not forget. We must always keep God's loving compassion vital and alive in our congregation and individual discipleship. It's the flip side of this miracle, but perhaps the most important for us today. Luke wanted us to know the power of Jesus to deal with death and that Jesus was even more compassionate than the great prophets of old. That's great news from Nain — but let us be compassionate as well.

Mercy On
The Wrong Day

Luke 13:10-17

To the bent-over crippled in the spirit on a Sabbath,
Jesus gave the gift of upright posture restored.
In him is a wonderful freedom for people over laws.
Here is a warning lest we crave power instead of mercy.

I've received only one reprimand for wrong behavior in my forty years of ordained ministry. I'm pretty sure you would like to know what I had done which violated the sensibilities of my congregation and shepherd. I was in my first parish, Third Lutheran Church, Springfield, Ohio, where they numbered the congregations one though five as they were organized.

It was Easter Sunday afternoon. Lent and Holy Week were finished, Jesus was out of the grave, and my work load looked to be a little more manageable. In that spirit, three of our sons and I decided we would take our newly acquired, double-engine go-cart out to the track for a few rounds. When we got there, they were organizing a rather major race. I entered it on a whim. I won third place! Next day on the sports page was the comment that "local pastor of Third caps third place in third race at the track."

Not all of the congregation celebrated our near victory. A group in the church who were angry over the successful integration of the congregation's black neighbors were especially incensed that their pastor would take part in such a sport on the day of resurrection. The ensuing letter from my Bishop, Herbert Veler, hung for years on the wall in my study. It was a gentle reprimand from a loving bishop.

Of course Luke, a doctor, tells a different story. There weren't any go-cart tracks open in Palestine. Besides, Easter hadn't come yet. Still, it's my guess that of all the disciples, Peter and Mary Magdalene probably would have made excellent competitive race drivers!

Jesus was still preaching in the synagogues, but just barely. Opposition to his message and claims was building. In this synagogue, Jesus noticed a woman bent over double who had been that way for eighteen years. Her contemporaries blamed it on demon possession. Today we might call the condition fusion of the spinal vertebrae. Jesus took the mercy-filled initiative. Luke tells it: "When Jesus saw her, he called her forward and said to her, 'Woman, you are set free from your infirmity!' Then he put his hands on her, and immediately she straightened up and praised God" (Luke 13:12-13).

While only Doctor Luke, who was very interested in any of Jesus' healings, tells the delightful story of a day when something really happened in church, we still find it instructive and inspiring. I especially focus right in on Luke's words that this woman was "... crippled by a spirit ..." (Luke 13:11). That was surely a hint that on that particular day everyone believed that to be ill or have a deformity was to be possessed by Satan and/or demons.

But the words "crippled by a spirit" intrigue me about our lives now 2,000 years later and within our church also. Aren't we all from time to time crippled by a spirit? There are still spirits which can distort us from the way we ought to be. The Bible warns us of some of them: "The cravings of sinful people, the lust of their eyes, and the boasting of what they have and do ..." (1 John 2:16). It warns us of a spirit of greed which can addict us to wealth and put us in bondage of getting and keeping money.

And we must mention how we get all wrapped up in the fear of what other people will think of us. That one has kept so many of us as spiritual runts when God would have us be giants. The spirits called alcohol and drugs. The spirits of a jealousy which can tear our relationships apart. The spirits of suspicion which infect working together with other well-meaning and motivated people. And, of course, there is that spirit of "me first" and self-centeredness which reduces our human nature to one of being bent over in conniving and manipulation. Then there is the seductive, distorting spirit of power over others. We'll save that one for the synagogue president a little later on.

At Third Lutheran many years ago there may have been the spirit of racism and ugly prejudice at work, as well as a brash, young, insensitive pastor racing a twin-engine go-cart on Easter Sunday afternoon.

We were not created by God to be possessed and crippled by these spirits which distort our stature. Today Jesus says to us as well as to the woman bent over for eighteen years, "... you are set free from your infirmity" (Luke 13:12b).

Not only are there spirits which cripple us, but there is a new sense of freedom available when we give ourselves to Christ and his ministry. It's not easy to describe: freedom, relief from guilt and worry, confidence we are okay, courage to face the future, the stuff necessary to deal with it, liberty. So like that bent-over woman, we can stand tall again.

In the little town of Eisleben, Germany, where the great reformer Martin Luther was born and died, there is in the church tower a collection of his books. On a page of his Bible (which has a piece of chain still connected to it) written in large letters in the margin are the words, "Free indeed." It marks chapter 8 of John: "So if the Son sets you free, you will be free indeed" (v. 36).

Jesus going to the cross for our undeserved forgiveness, coming out of the grave so we might also, and returning in spirit to equip us for life here with his presence, is freeing. We are free indeed. We need not be bent over in weariness, or guilt, or addiction, or worry any longer. For Jesus puts his hands on us here, too, and we can straighten up and walk out into our lives this week as God's free children.

On the face of it, what happened next seems so silly. Jesus heals a faithful member who was all bent out of shape for eighteen years and the president of the congregation and some members, instead of rejoicing, complain! Shades of the other miracles where, instead of celebrating their gift to the one who needed it, some grouchy, grumpy, suspicious, old men complain and attack. The man let down through Peter's mother-in-law's roof is a good example.

What is it that makes us this way? We just believe it's too good to be true, or we're suspicious it was all faked, or jealous of whatever was done for them, or can't stand the attention they got and we didn't? Here the complaint was that Jesus was working on the Sabbath. And, of course, everyone knew it was against the rules to do that.

It's a warning not to put rules above concern and mercy for people. We must always guard against making our religion a whole bunch of "Thou shalt nots ..." Mercy must always take precedence over rules and interpretation of laws. So the rule was to keep holy the Sabbath. Certainly giving back this woman's stature was much more important and holy that day than refraining from offending a minute law about what is work and what isn't.

In Christianity the individual must always come before the system. We must never sacrifice the personal compassion for individuals which Jesus wants us to have for them for the sake of greater numbers or larger effort's success.

In addition to Luke's wanting us to know of another healing Jesus did, I think he also wanted us to see clearly how it is when the kingdom comes into the middle of a congregation. A woman who had been all bent over for eighteen years stood up straight and the people "... were delighted with all the wonderful things he was doing" (Luke 13:17b). So many dramatic and dynamic changes took place that day because Jesus was in their midst. The kingdom was there and that rearranged lives and people and even the Sabbath rules everyone thought could never ever be changed!

So here in our congregation, as we pray for and expect the kingdom to come, we can expect such things as mean people to be much kinder, racism turned into loving discipleship, broken marriages brought back together, alcoholics made sober, drug addicts made clean, egocentrics turned to humble care givers, demanding and abusive parents changed to loving mentors, worriers freed up and encouraged, and depressed lifted up with new hope. That's the way it ought to be and can be, as Dr. Luke wanted us to know and experience the results of the kingdom of God breaking through here as well. It was the same synagogue, the same bent-over woman, the same congregation, the same congregational president. But it was a new preacher with a new and different message — about the kingdom, and healing, and power over evil. It was the dynamite power of God's presence. That little church will never be the same again. Luke knew that and wrote it down.

The flip side of this miracle might be about *a president hooked on control and power; it could be about the need to break some old traditions which prohibit our witness; or it just might be encouragement to expect miracles here in our congregation.* We've heard the main teachings of the miracle of healing in the synagogue on Sabbath, but there are always some sides or subtly under-items which are fun to examine.

I'm not sure we come to church expecting enough (or actually wanting enough) to happen. The breaking-in of the kingdom of God is not something we talk about a lot these days. I doubt if we sit very often on the edge of our pew watching around us for a miracle to happen before, during, or after the sermon. But it could, if we pray for it and have faith. Often what God can do here is severely limited to what we believe and expect. God's always ready, but we aren't.

The breaking-in of the kingdom, in fact all preaching, now seems to be limited by the view of kingdom in the sweet by-and-by, way down the road from the present. Still God invites us as he did that woman for action now. He calls us forward *now* as he called her *then*. And he offers to give us new stature and a healthy taste of kingdom here and now.

I'm eager to point out something else to you today. The flip side of this story must also be about power. That president of the synagogue was angry not so much because Jesus broke a rule on keeping the Sabbath. This authority lost control of the situation. He probably had invited the now famous wonder-worker and Nazarene preacher to be the guest speaker. He was sure to boost attendance for that Sabbath. But Jesus went far beyond what the president expected him to do. He took over! Suddenly all eyes were on Jesus and not on the president. Jesus' power was so much stronger. His mercy was so much more attractive than the man's regulations and rules. He was furious because he lost power. We get that way if we have allowed our sinful thirst for power over people to enslave us to its bloated lifestyle. It is in humility we find kingdom power and the love of people rather than control and manipulation of people. That's God's way. That's power also. Jesus had it and the synagogue president did not.

We all must examine ourselves over and over because we remain imperfect and sinners; we must deal with each other and others with whom we live, work, and play, not out of the position of being over them, but in love, being with them and sharing the creative power which God gives.

There is one other part of the flip side of this miracle: Every congregation, no matter how faithful and devout, needs miracles. Because we are a gathering of forgiven sinners, we still aren't very good at dealing with each other. The harder we all work at our discipleship, the more we rub each other the wrong way and tramp on each other's toes. We need over and over the miracle of renewed trust and love for each other.

Consider what the miracles we need as a group of Christians trying to be faithful disciples are. Here are some I will pray for:

— That Jesus would give us a new boldness so we will all go from here and witness to others about the good news we know.

— That Jesus would convince us to be a lot better at sharing our money with the mission and ministry of our church.

— That Jesus would equip each of us to be ministers all this week long wherever we find ourselves.

— That Jesus would make us people of prayer so we might continue to grow in depth of faith.

— That Jesus would turn us from skeptical, cynical, critical members to loving, grace-filled ones who bless others by our presence.

— That Jesus would help us stand tall again as he did that woman in the synagogue that day, if we are bent over with burdens and worry.

Perhaps that's enough miracle working this week, but next Sabbath may Jesus work the miracle that all of us be here together expecting great things again.

Regardless of the congregation's consternation about Sabbath rules that day, I'm confident there was one family in the Palestine village where the hostess stood up straight for the first time in a long time and told of her great joy.

Add this flip side to the traditional side of the kingdom coming now, putting love of individual over enforcement of rules, the gift of being set free, and being cured of those spirits which cripple us, and you have a marvelous story for Palestine and promise for us, too.